Table of Contents

READING

Letter Review 4
Long Vowels 6
Short Vowels 28
Consonant Blends and Digraphs 48

READING GAMES AND PUZZLES

Letter Review 62
Vowels and Consonants 67
Long Vowels 72
Short Vowels 83
Long and Short Vowel Review 98
Consonant Blends and Digraphs 101

LANGUAGE

Sentences 112
Plurals 125
Contractions 129
ABC Order 133
Compound Words 135
Verbs Forms and Word Usage 139
Synonyms, Antonyms and Homophones 144
Consonant Blends and Digraphs 101
Writing Sentences and Stories 149

Table of Contents

MATH

Size and Shape Comparisons 162
Counting 1 to 10 166
More Than, Less Than and Equal To 170
Counting 177
Addition and Subtraction 182
Even/Odd 192
Place Value 196
Estimation 202
Money 206
Graphing 216
Story Problems/Addition and Subtraction 226
Probability and Combinations 239
Time 242
Ordinal Numbers 249
Shapes 253
Multiplication 260
Division 274
Advanced Multiplication 277
Fractions 280

MATH GAMES AND PUZZLES

Tic-Tac-Toe Games 292
Codes 303
Patterns, Mazes and Logic Puzzles 307

READING

Recognition of Letters

In each box, draw a line from the capital letters to the small letters. The first one is done for you.

For each picture below, write the consonant it begins with on the line. The first one is done for you.

S

_____   _____   _____   _____   _____

_____   _____   _____   _____   _____

_____   _____   _____   _____   _____

_____   _____   _____   _____   _____

Long ā

Here is Abe's safe. It only holds things that have the **long ā** sound, such as **cape** and **game**. Look at the pictures below. Color the things that might be in the safe.

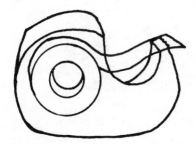

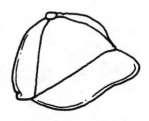

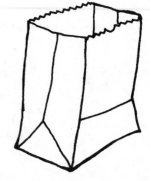

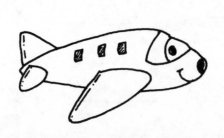

Abe wrote words that have the **long ā** sound. Draw a line from each word to its matching picture.

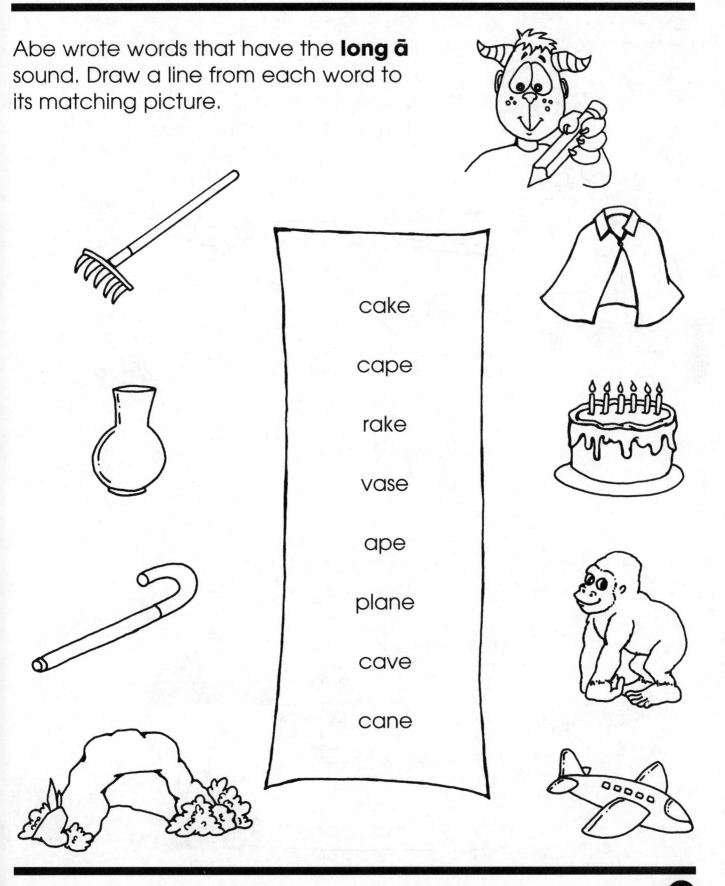

cake

cape

rake

vase

ape

plane

cave

cane

Long ā

Help the monsters get to the cave before it rains. Circle the name of each picture on the path. Then, write the names on the lines.

_____
can   cane

_____
rake   rate

_____
tap   tape

_____
ape   add

_____
vase   vine

_____
plan   plane

_____
cat   cage

Spike has many kites. Each one has a picture of something that has the **long ī** sound in its name, such as **dime**. Look at the kites below. Color the ones that belong to Spike.

Long ī

Help Spike hike down the hill. Write the word for each picture on the path. Use the words on the clouds.

pie   dime
bike   hive

fire   kite
tire   mice

_____

_____

_____

_____

_____

_____

_____

Read Spike's riddles. The answer to each riddle is a **long ī** word. Write the answers on the lines. Use the words in the box.

nine	tire	hive	rice
pine	fire	bike	prize

1. This is on a car. _____

2. Bees live here. _____

3. This is very hot. _____

4. This is a number. _____

5. You can ride this. _____

6. This is a tree. _____

7. You can eat this. _____

8. You win this. _____

Find the pictures of the words you wrote. Draw a line from each word to its matching picture.

Long ō

Mo drew pictures of things around her home. **Mo** and **home** have the **long ō** sound. Color each picture that has the **long ō** sound in its name.

Help Mo get home. Color the pictures that have **long ō** in their names to make a path for her.

hoe

mop

pole

sock

rope

rose

hole

rock

top

box

log

hose

pot

doll

note

phone

lock

clock

cone

robe

bone

Long ō

Read the riddles below. Write the answers on the lines. Use the **long ō** words that are in the smoke.

nose
rose
robe
stone

toe
home
bone
stove

1. You live here. _____

2. You cook on this. _____

3. This is a plant. _____

4. You smell with this. _____

5. This is a rock. _____

6. This is part of your foot. _____

7. A dog may hide this. _____

8. This is made of cloth. _____

Complete the words below.
Write **a** or **o** on the lines.
Then, read the words aloud.

r___se   t___pe   b___ne

c___ke   r___pe   r___ke

c___ne   v___se   h___se

p___le   c___ve   r___be

h___e   pl___ne   g___te

Long ī and ō

The monsters are going to eat something good. To find out what it is, color the shapes below. If a shape has a **long ī** word in it, color it green. If it has a **long ō** word in it, color it blue. Color all the other shapes yellow.

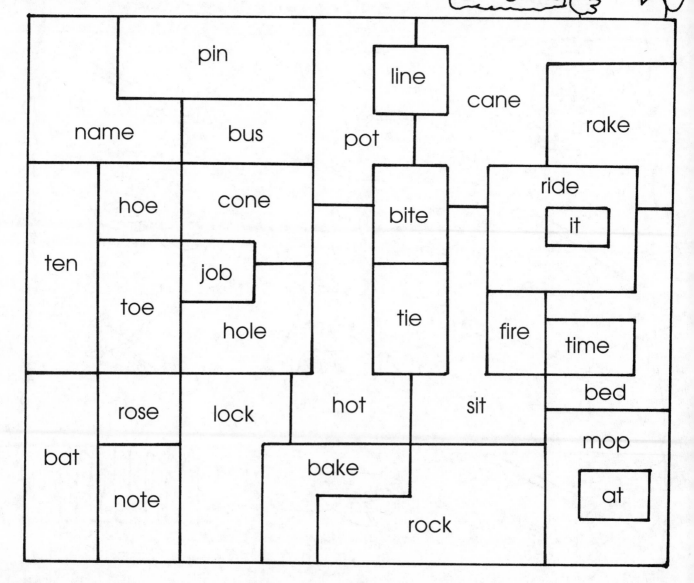

What are the monsters going to eat?_____

Lulu has a mule. The word **mule** has the **long ū** sound. Lulu's mule has a pack on his back. In it are things that have the **long ū** sound. Look at the pictures below. Color the things that might be in the pack.

glue

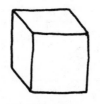

cup

tube

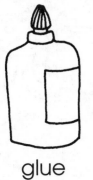

bug

cube

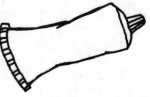

nut

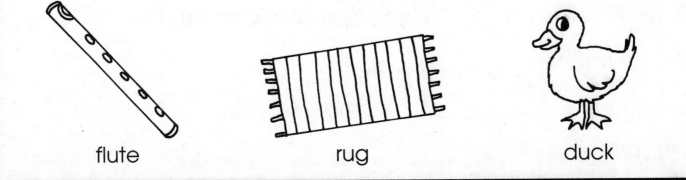

flute

rug

duck

Long ū

Complete the sentences below with **long ū** words. Use the words in the box. Then, read the story aloud.

| mule | tune | use | flute | huge | music |

1. Lulu plays her _____.

2. Spike hums a _____.

3. Mo likes to _____ a can for a drum.

4. Abe taps on a _____ box.

5. Lulu's _____ stamps his feet.

6. Everyone likes _____!

Read the list below. Draw a line from each description to its matching picture.

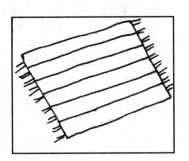

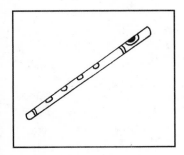

- a fine bike

- an ice cube

- a long tube

- five mice

- a huge truck

- a wide rug

- six cute bugs

- a thin flute

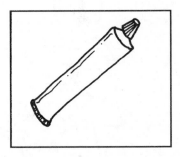

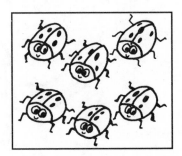

ai Words

Help Abe make a chain of **ai** words. Write **ai** on the lines below.
Then, say the words aloud. Listen to the **long ā** sound.

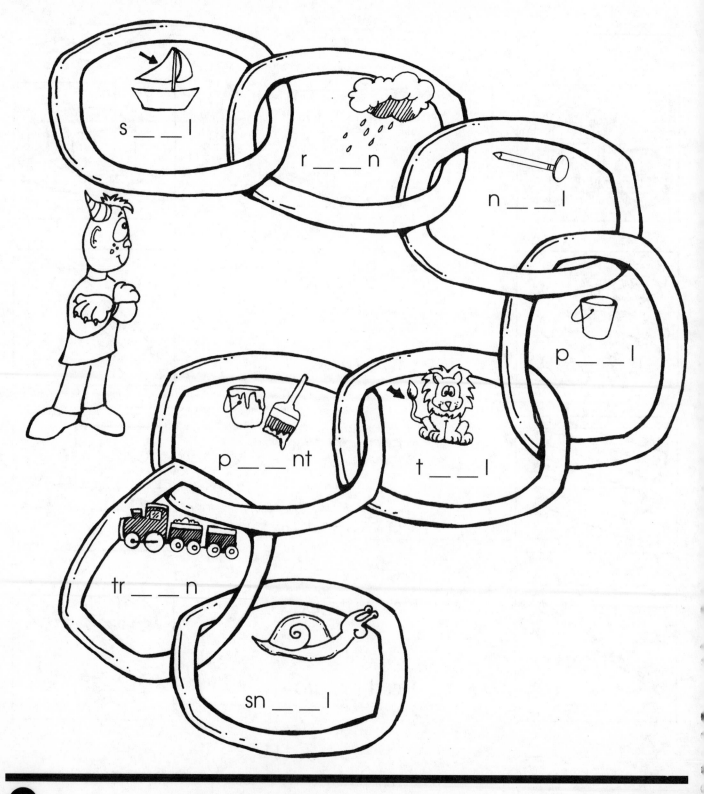

s _ _ l

r _ _ _ n

n _ _ _ l

p _ _ _ l

p _ _ nt

t _ _ l

tr _ _ n

sn _ _ _ l

Look at the picture and the words below. Each **ay** word in the box has the **long ā** sound. Say the words aloud. Then, use the words to complete the sentences.

| day | jay | hay | stays | gray | crayons |

1. It is a rainy _____.

2. Abe _____ at home.

3. He gets out a box of _____.

4. Abe draws a _____ mule.

5. The mule is eating some _____.

6. A blue _____ is looking at the mule.

ee Words

Deek made a list of **long ē** words. Each word has the letters **ee**. Read the words and write each one under the correct picture below.

tree	seed	weed
bee	eel	sleep
feet	wheel	sheep

_____

_____

_____

_____

_____

_____

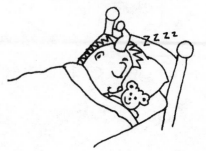

_____

_____

_____

Sometimes the letters **ea** make the **long ē** sound. Write **ea** on the lines to complete the words below. Then, find the pictures of the **ea** words in the beach scene and color them.

l _ _ f   p _ _ s   _ _ gle

s _ _ l   b _ _ ds   p _ _ nut

oa Words

The letters **oa** make the **long ō** sound. Read the words on Mo's boat. Circle the letters **oa** in each word. Then, use the words to complete the sentences.

coat	road	soap	roast
goat	toad	float	toast

1. A _____ has horns.

2. Mom will _____ the meat.

3. A _____ looks like a frog.

4. Mo likes to eat _____ and jam.

5. I will hang up my _____.

6. I can see six cars on the _____.

7. A boat can _____.

8. I wash my face with _____.

Help the monsters fly through the clouds. Complete the words below by writing **a**, **i**, **o** or **u** on the lines.

r___pe

k___te

g___te

t___be

f___re

c___be

r___se

h___ve

h___se

r___ke

c___ve

m___le

Long Vowels

Look at the vowel sign each monster is holding. Then, look at the snake beside the monster. Read the words on it. Color only the parts of the snake that have words with the matching vowel sound.

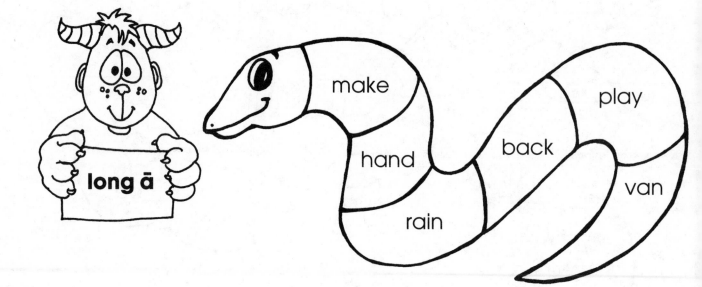

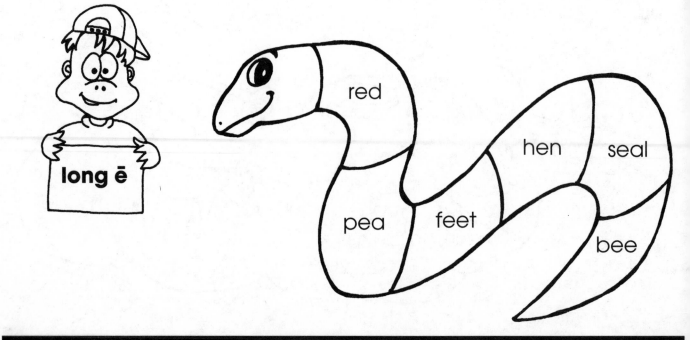

long ī

ride
bite
time
mile
pie
pin

long ō

hot
hole
road
boat
sock
toe

long ū

sun
nut
cute
mule
run
use

ă   ĕ   ĭ   ŏ   ŭ

căt   ĕlf   pĭg   ŏtter   dŭck

Say the name of each picture below. Write the **short vowel** you hear on the lines.

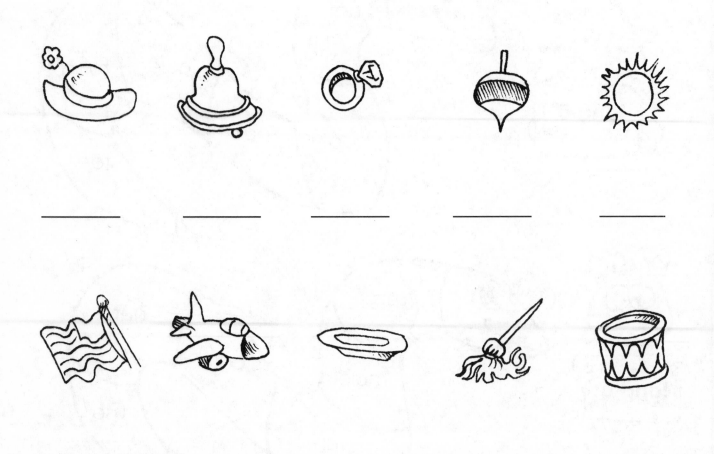

_____   _____   _____   _____   _____

_____   _____   _____   _____   _____

Pam likes hamburgers! You can make words that rhyme with **am**. Pick a letter from the box and write it in the lines.

y   P
c   j
r   h
l   st

"Hamburger" has a short ă sound!

Dan prefers sandwiches. Pick a letter from the box to fill in the sandwiches to make words that rhyme with **an**.

"Sandwich" has a short ă sound, too!

f   D
c   m
r   st
h   s

Short ă

Matt is a rat, and he lives in a saggy bag. Look at
the **at** and **ag** words below and say the ones with pictures.
Then, fill in the blanks with letters from the box. Do all the **at**
words rhyme? Do all the **ag** words rhyme?

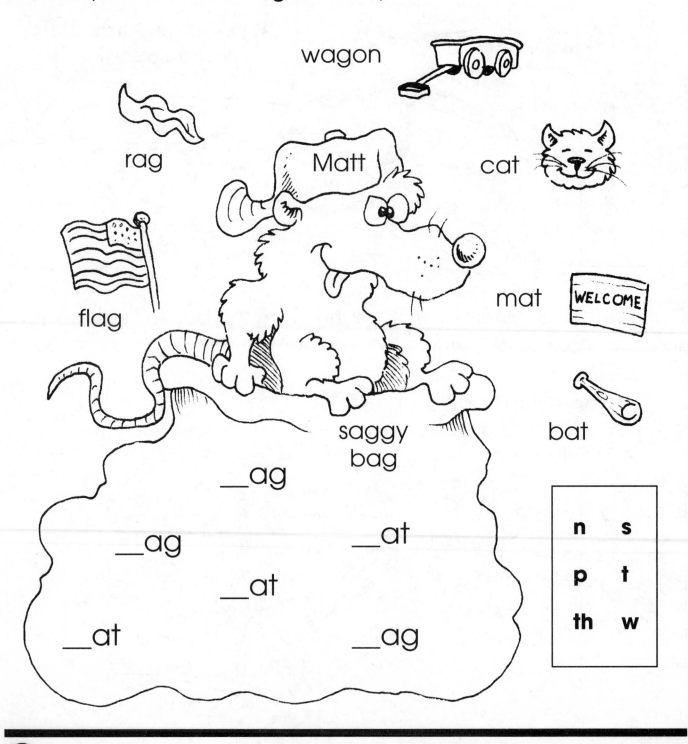

wagon

rag

cat

Matt

flag

mat

WELCOME

bat

saggy
bag

__ag

__ag

__at

__at

__at

__ag

n	s
p	t
th	w

Use the box below to help you catch these **short ĕ** words. Then, fill in the letters on the lines.

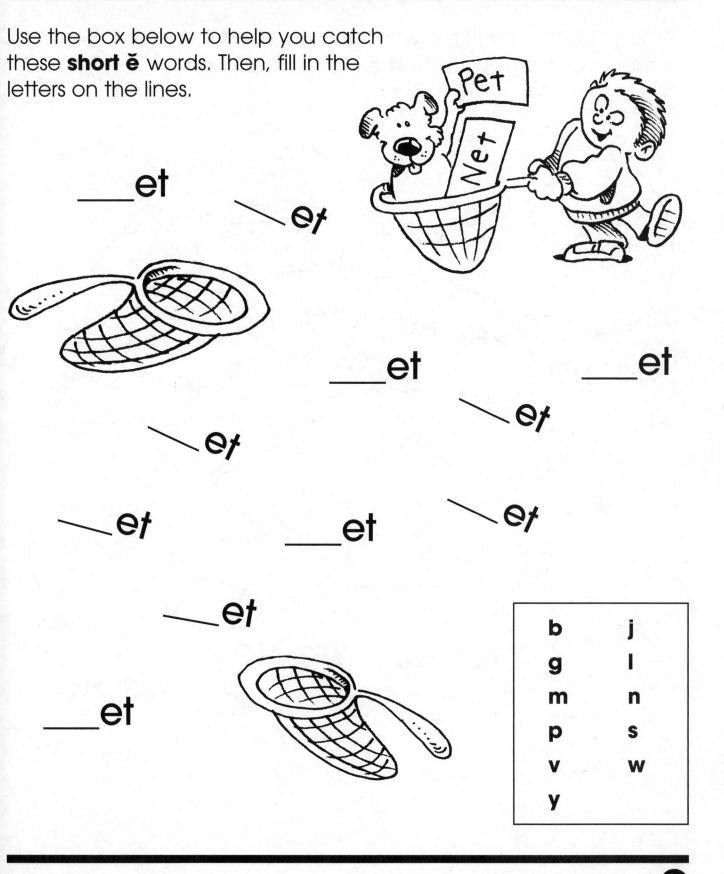

__et

__et

__et   __et

__et

__et

__et   __et

__et

__et

b	j
g	l
m	n
p	s
v	w
y	

Short ĕ

Circle **yes** under each picture that has a **short ĕ** sound. If the picture does not have a **short ĕ** sound, circle **no**.

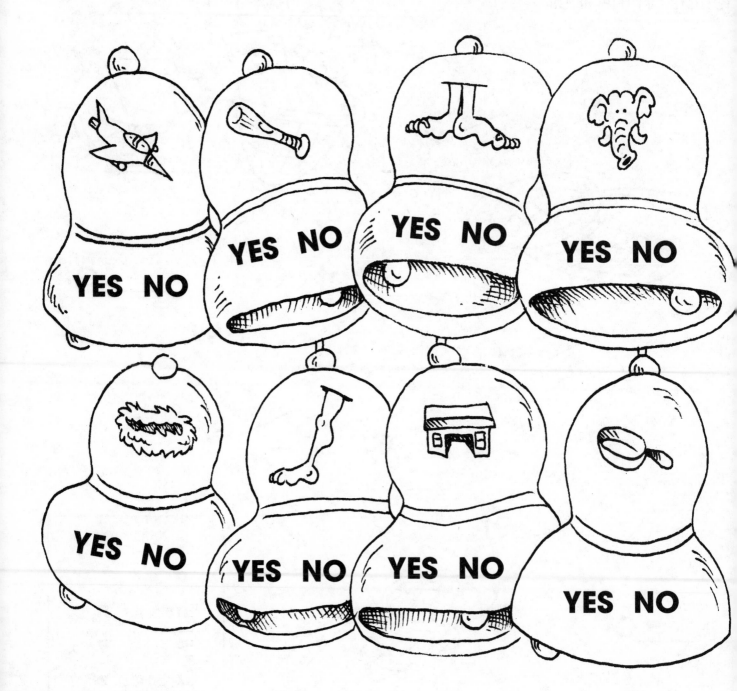

YES NO

YES NO

YES NO

YES NO

YES NO

YES NO

YES NO

YES NO

Jenny the Hen is building a nest for her many eggs. You can fill her eggs for her with **short ĕ** words from the box. The polka dot eggs each get an **en** word. The striped eggs get an **est** word.

best	test	hen
rest	pen	ten
west	zest	den
nest	men	Ben
pest	vest	

Short ă and ĕ

Tic-tac-toe can help you review the **short ă** and **short ĕ** vowel sounds. Draw a line through any three matching vowel sounds in a row. Remember that a line can be diagonal ($\nearrow\searrow$).

GAME 1

GAME 2

Vinnie is a fish. So is Minnie. Their names both have the **short ĭ** sound. Vinnie and Minnie are swimming with lots of **short ĭ** words below. Say each word pair out loud and cross out the ones that do not rhyme.

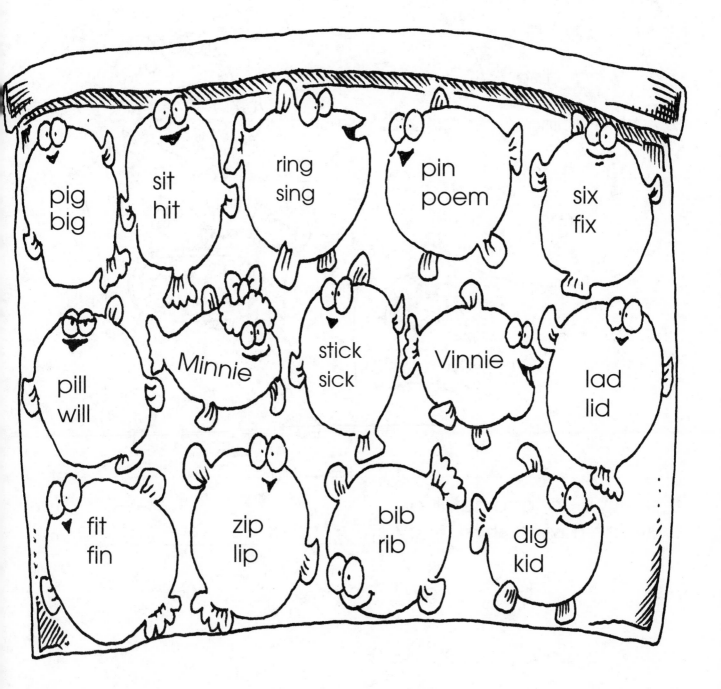

Short ĭ

The king is singing words that rhyme with **ing**! Help him sing out this rhyming set of words.

sing   ring

wing   ding

thing   cling

zing   ping

bring

The king is up to something!
Write the missing **short ĭ** vowels to find out what he is doing.

He _____s br_____ng_____ng a r_____ng to

the s_____ng_____ng queen!

Use the box to fill in the missing consonants to make whole **it** words. Then, write your own **it** words on the baseballs.

b	f
h	k
l	p
qu	s
w	sk

__it

___

___

___

___

__it

___

__it

___

___

Short Ĭ

Billy and Millie love to wiggle as they dance the jig. Circle the words below which rhyme with **ig** or **ill**. Then, cross out the words that do not rhyme.

Ollie the Octopus is juggling boxes again! Ollie's name has a **short ŏ** in it, and more **short ŏ** words are in Ollie's boxes. In each box, circle the word that goes with the picture and write it on the line.

Short ŏ

You can help Ollie add to his collection of **short ŏ** words. Circle the word in each row that names the picture in the box. Cross out the word in each row that contains a long vowel.

pop   hop   mop   rope   top   cop

block   rock   sock   soak   lock   clock

log   jog   dog   go   fog   frog

dot   hot   note   pot   lot   got

Fill in the missing consonants below. Then, write other **op** words on the lines.

Now, fill in the lines to make **ock** words to go with the pictures. What words did you make?

1. s___ ___ ___   2. cl___ ___ ___   3. l___ ___ ___   4. r___ ___ ___

Short ŏ

It's silly rhyme time! Fill in the lines with the **short ŏ** endings shown. If you need help, look at the picture clues.

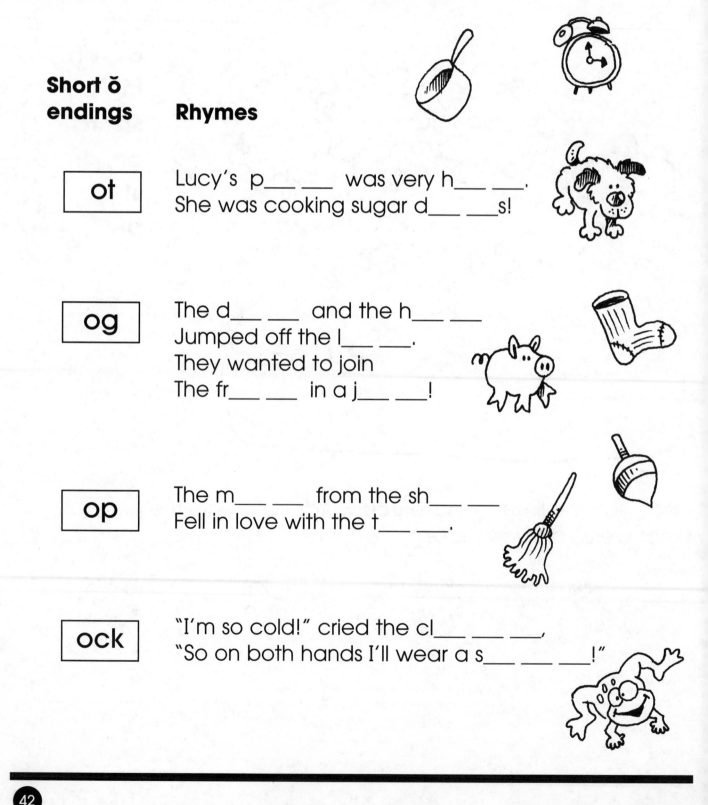

Short ŏ endings

Rhymes

ot

Lucy's p___ ___ was very h___ ___.
She was cooking sugar d___ ___s!

og

The d___ ___ and the h___ ___
Jumped off the l___ ___.
They wanted to join
The fr___ ___ in a j___ ___!

op

The m___ ___ from the sh___ ___
Fell in love with the t___ ___.

ock

"I'm so cold!" cried the cl___ ___ ___,
"So on both hands I'll wear a s___ ___ ___!"

Hurry and get under the umbrella, because it's raining **short ŭ** words! Color the raindrops that have the **short ŭ** vowel sound.

Look carefully in the rug—there are lots of snug little bugs! Use the consonants to the left to make **ug** words. The first one is done for you.

d m h
b j t
pl

dug

Draw a line through any row down (↓) or across (→) that has the same **short vowel** sound.

Which short vowel sounds made a row? _____

Which short vowel sounds made a row? _____

Short Vowels

In each flower petal, write a word with the correct short vowel sound. Use all the words in the box below.

duck	sun	box	log	web	mop
fan	egg	ring	nut	fish	zip
hand	cap	leg	bat	rug	bell
bug	pill	gum	pen	dog	pig
rock	lip	bag	cat	sock	bed

Read each word below. Color the rocket red if the word has a long vowel. Then, write which long vowel you hear (ā, ē, ī, ō or ū). If the vowel sound is short, color the rocket blue, and write which short vowel you hear (ă, ĕ, ĭ, ŏ or ŭ).

vowel sound   **vowel sound**

lid _____   rain _____

boot _____   duck _____

fish _____   rock _____

bell _____   pie _____

rake _____   bag _____

key _____   toe _____

What a mess! Drake the Dragon has dropped a lot of **r blends** on his cave floor. R blends are consonants combined with an **r** to make a special sound.

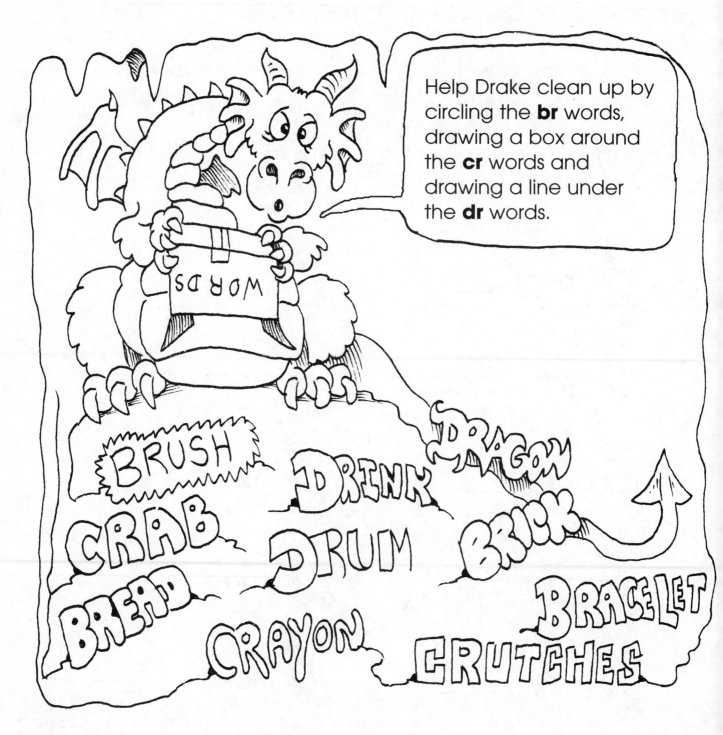

Help Drake clean up by circling the **br** words, drawing a box around the **cr** words and drawing a line under the **dr** words.

Follow the frog's trail, and say the name of each picture. Then, on the line, write the **r blend** you hear—**fr**, **gr**, **pr** or **tr**.

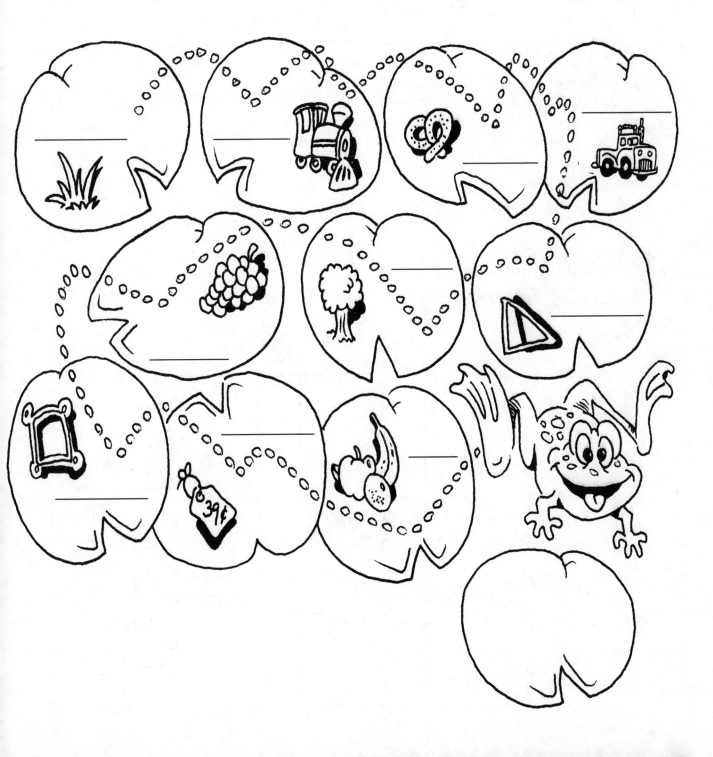

Fill in the crossword puzzle with **r blend** words. Use the pictures at the start of each word as clues.

Look at these **l blends** below and on page 52. **L blends** combine a consonant with an **l** to make a special sound. Mark the different blends you see as follows:

bl blends ☆

cl blends ✗

fl blends ●

gl blends ○

pl blends ✓

sl blends ♀

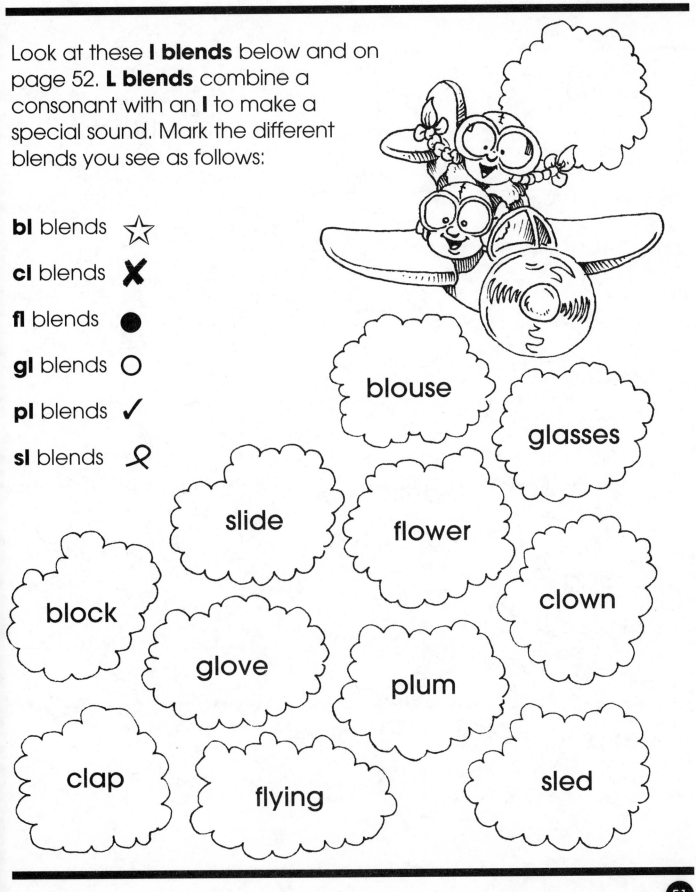

blouse

glasses

slide

flower

clown

block

glove

plum

clap

flying

sled

cloud

blue

plant

plane

slipper

glow

blanket

floppy

clothes

flag

sleep

plate

glide

Say the name of each **I blend** picture. Then, write the blend on the line in each flag.

s Consonant Blends

Each step below has a picture of a word with an **s blend**. Fill in the box with the **s blend** that goes with the picture. The first one is done for you.

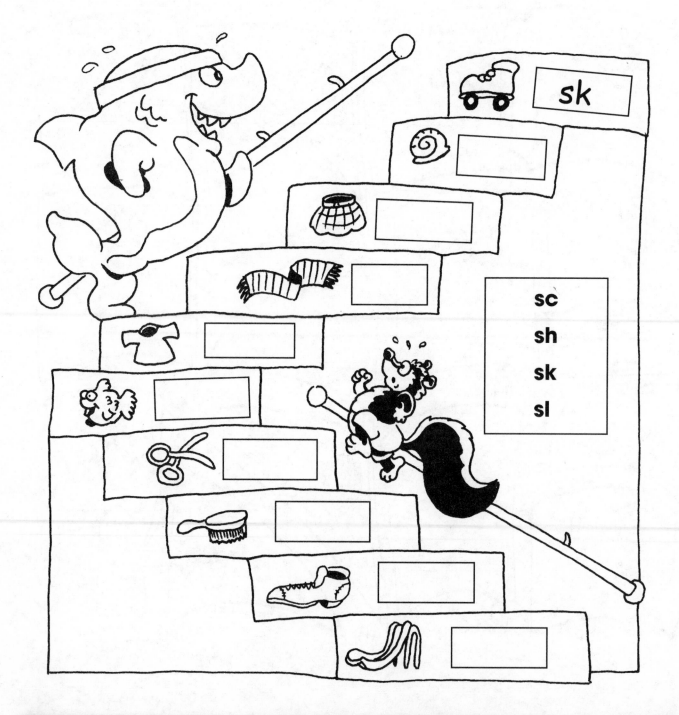

Look who is racing down the stairs—the snail and the spider! Who do you think will win? Each step below has a picture of word with an **s blend**. Fill in the box with the **s blend** that goes with the picture.

sm
sn
sp
st

s Consonant Blends

Fill in the missing **s blends** below.

___eater

___ing

___an

___im

___ing

___inkler

___ash

___raw

___ray

___ong

These special stamps each contain an **s blend** picture. Write the **s blend** you hear on the line in each stamp.

Consonant Blends

Circle the correct **blend** below each picture.

gr pr tr

pl gl sl

sh sw sn

gr cr dr

sl st sk

pl gl bl

sw sh st

sk sp sl

pr tr gr

sn sw sc

sl sc sp

tr fr cr

dr br tr

pr br dr

sk sw sh

pl cl fl

A **digraph** is a combination of a consonant with the letter **h** to make a special sound.

Here are four digraphs:

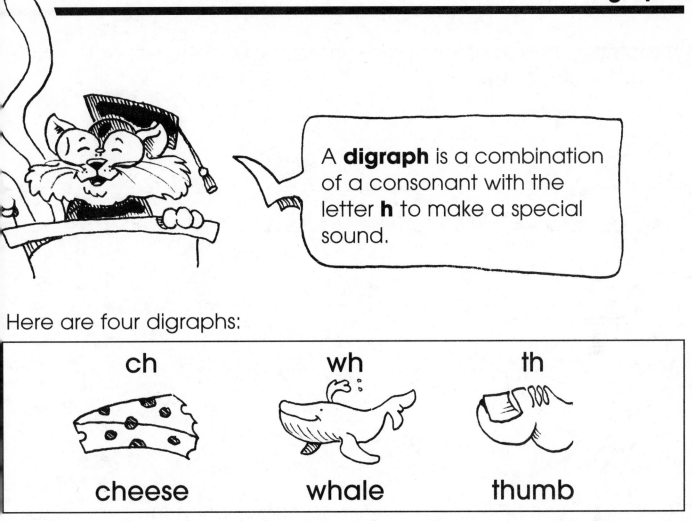

ch	wh	th
cheese	whale	thumb

Now, match the **digraph** word on the left to its picture on the right. Draw a line to connect them.

church

wheelbarrow

thorn

Digraphs

To complete each of these silly sentences, fill in the correct digraph—**ch**, **sh**, **th** or **wh**.

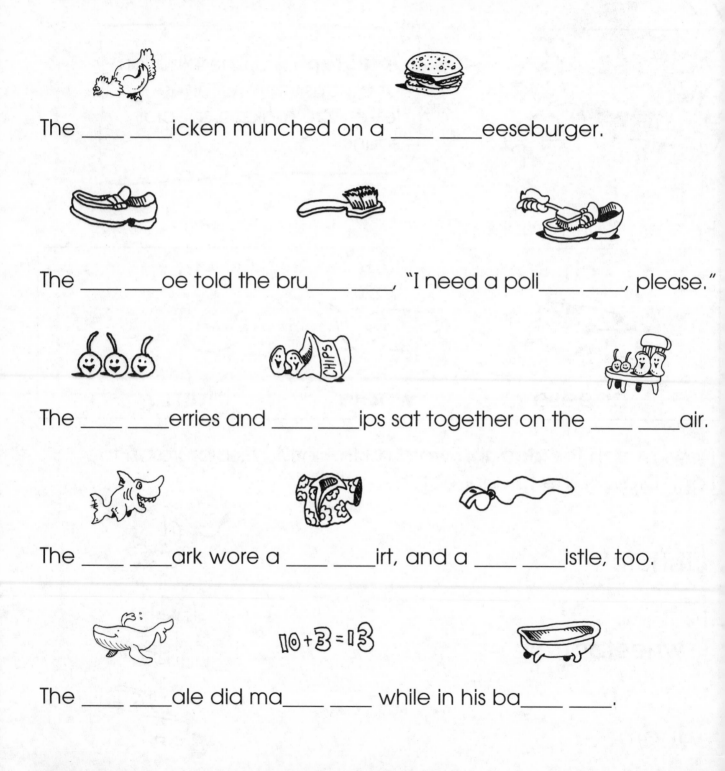

The ____ ____icken munched on a ____ ____eeseburger.

The ____ ____oe told the bru____ ____, "I need a poli____ ____, please."

The ____ ____erries and ____ ____ips sat together on the ____ ____air.

The ____ ____ark wore a ____ ____irt, and a ____ ____istle, too.

The ____ ____ale did ma____ ____ while in his ba____ ____.

READING GAMES AND PUZZLES

Upper- and Lowercase Letters

The noodles in this bowl of soup are shaped like the letters of the alphabet. Some letters of the alphabet are missing. Say the alphabet out loud. Circle each letter in the soup as you say it. When you come to a missing letter, write it in the bowl. Be sure to make all the letters **uppercase**, or **capitals**.

On the last page, all the letters in the soup were uppercase. Now, it is your turn to make a bowl of "lowercase-letter soup." Inside the bowl, write the whole alphabet in **lowercase**, or **small** letters. If you need help writing your letters, look at the letters on the tablecloth.

Upper- and Lowercase Letters

Darrel needs to put all the **uppercase** letters in one barrel and all the **lowercase** letters in the other barrel. Help him by drawing a line from each letter on his sign below to the barrel in which that letter belongs.

In the puzzle below, color each square that contains a **lowercase** letter.

Row 1	I	o	Y	N	M	w	e	r
Row 2	M	c	a	B	D	s	e	Z
Row 3	N	E	R	I	C	U	G	F
Row 4	C	Y	F	I	e	H	D	M
Row 5	J	P	S	t	t	R	V	K
Row 6	W	O	I	D	B	T	X	A
Row 7	e	r	s	P	S	a	r	e
Row 8	c	o	F	A	W	Y	o	I

Upper- and Lowercase Letters

Circle all the **uppercase** letters on the
envelope below.

Miss Susan Small
12345 Alphabet Lane
Capital City, Kansas 00000

How many did you circle? _____

Amanda is having a block party, and she is inviting you to come. The consonant blocks are all piled up below, but some of the consonants are missing. Help Amanda by writing in the missing letters on the blank blocks. Be sure to use **uppercase** letters.

Vowels and Consonants

On this page, Amanda has piled up her vowel blocks. Write one vowel on each block. Be sure to put the **vowels** in alphabetical order, but this time use **lowercase** letters.

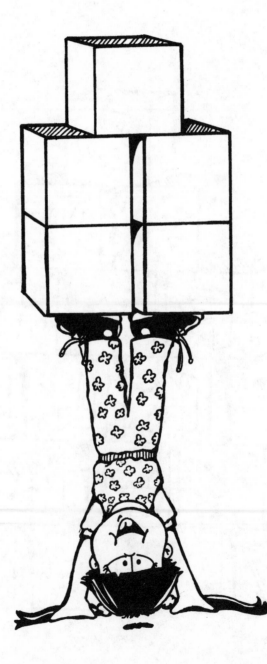

Each word below is missing a vowel. Complete the puzzle by filling in the missing **vowels**. Use each **vowel** only once. Some words go across (⟶) the puzzle. Other words go down (↓). The pictures will help you.

Vowels and Consonants

The puzzle box below has seven rows of squares that contain vowels and consonants. Go from left to right (→), saying the name of each letter in the row. When you come to a **consonant**, color in that square with your favorite color crayon.

Row 1	B	V	X	L	C	N	P
Row 2	A	O	I	R	E	U	O
Row 3	E	I	U	D	A	I	E
Row 4	O	E	A	G	O	E	U
Row 5	I	A	O	K	I	O	A
Row 6	E	U	I	Z	E	A	I
Row 7	U	O	E	C	A	I	O

Read each animal's name on the pages below. If the first letter of the name is a **vowel**, draw a square around that letter. If the first letter is a **consonant**, draw a triangle around it.

Zebra

Elephant

Bear

Ostrich

Ape

Otter

Long ā

Long vowels always sound like their names. Say the letter **a**. That is the **long ā** sound. Draw a line from each **long ā** word with the picture that shows what it means.

plane

lady

flame

ape

wave

spray

braid

hay

Circle each **long ā** word in the trail below.

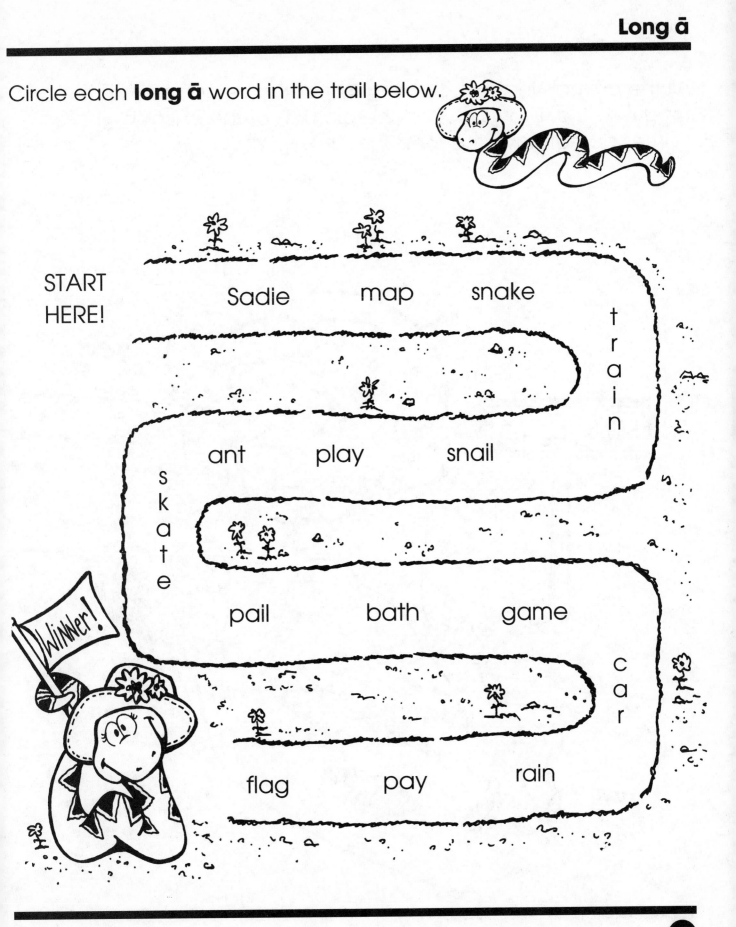

START HERE!

Sadie   map   snake

train

ant   play   snail

skate

pail   bath   game

car

flag   pay   rain

Winner!

Long ē

All the animals that live on **Long Ē** Street have names with the **long ē** sound. Draw an **X** on the pictures of the animals whose names do not have the **long ē** sound.

Now, use crayons to color the **long ē** animals any way you like.

Long ī

Ride the **long ī** spiral from the inside out. Fill in the letter **i** to make the **long ī** sound in each word. Say each word out loud as you go.

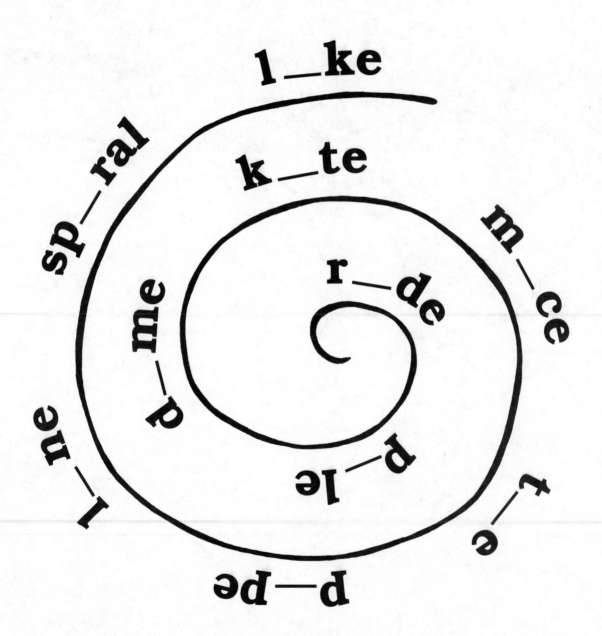

l_ke

k_te

m_ce

sp_ral

r_de

me

p_

p_le

t_e

l_ne

p_pe

I is a very short word that has the **long ī** sound. This game is called "What am I?" To play, read each clue written in the center of the page. Then, find the picture that answers the question "What am I?" Draw a line from each clue to the picture that it describes.

I shine.

I fry.

I slide.

I dry.

I bite.

I buy.

I fly.

I cry.

Long ō

Climb the **long ō** pole. As you go up, circle each word that has the **long ō** sound.

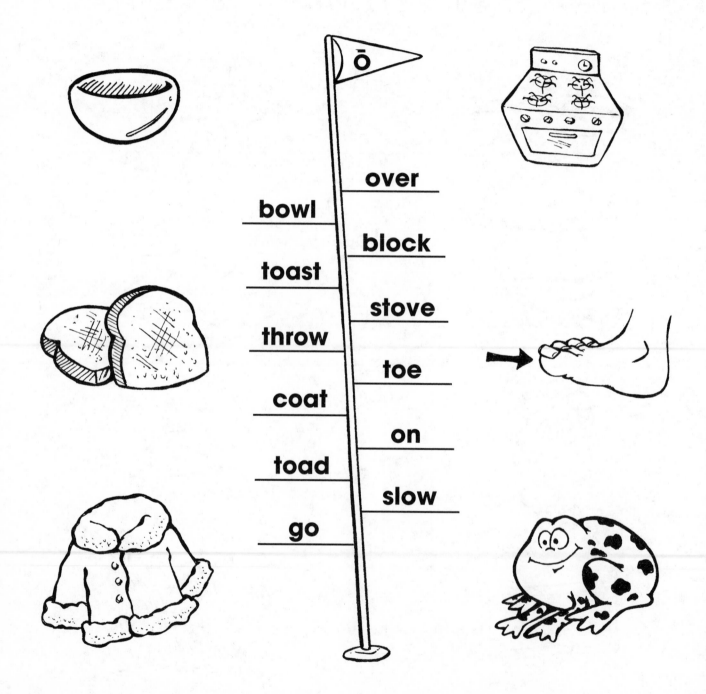

over

bowl

block

toast

stove

throw

toe

coat

on

toad

slow

go

Use the pictures in the box below to help you fill in the words in this **long ō** puzzle. The first one is done for you.

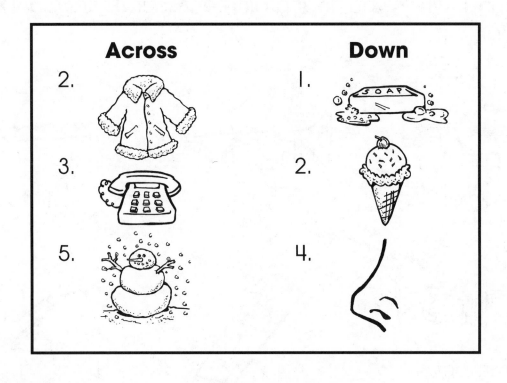

Long ū

Some of the musical instruments on this page have names with the **long ū** sound. Say the name of each instrument. Listen for the **long ū** sound. When you hear a different sound, draw an **X** over the picture.

ukulele

bugle

flute

trumpet

kazoo

bassoon

tuba

guitar

drum

Now, use your crayons to color the **long ū** instruments.

Look at the list of body parts below. Say each word out loud.
Then, write its long vowel sound on the line next to it: **ā, ē, ī, ō** or **ū**.
Draw a line from each word to that body part on the man. The first one is done for you.

face ___ā___

ear _____

nose _____

tooth _____

throat _____

shoulder _____

waist _____

nails _____

thigh _____

knee _____

elbow _____

heel _____

toes _____

In Mrs. Powell's long vowel store, she only sells clothes with names that have long vowels. Look at the clothes below. Say their names. Then, color the clothes that have **long vowel** names any way you like.

Short ă has the sound of the **a** in the name **Ann** and the words **hat** and **tap**. Look at the words and pictures. Say each word. Color each **short ă** picture. When you come to a word that has a different vowel sound, draw an **X** on that word and its picture.

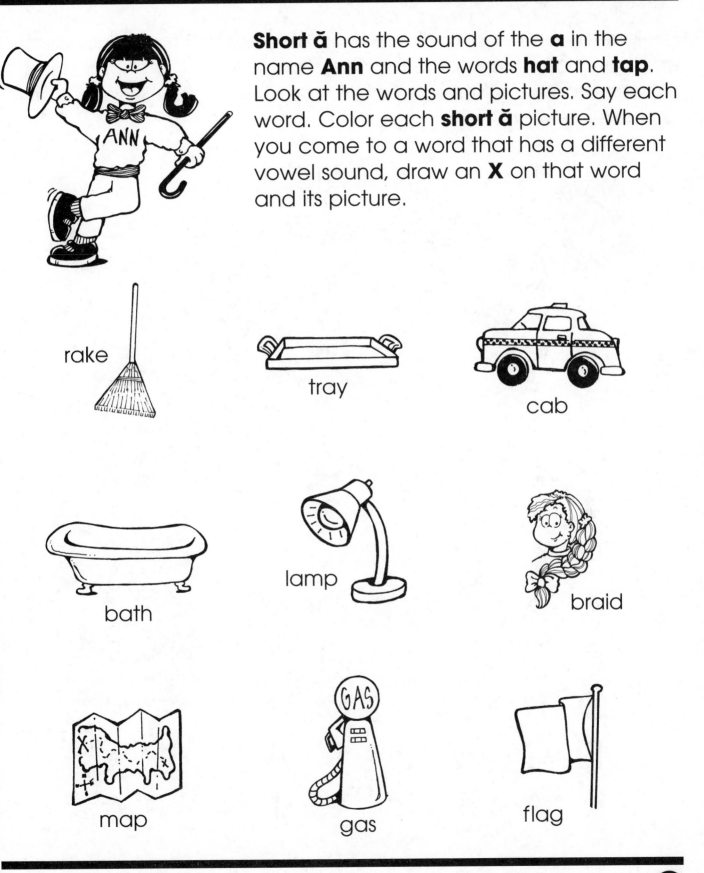

rake

tray

cab

bath

lamp

braid

map

gas

flag

Short ă

Look at the parade of animals marching around this page. Circle each animal whose name has the **short ă** sound. Then, find and circle the names of the animals in the puzzle below. Names can go across (⟶) or down (↓).

O K B A O B
H I C R B A
E C M A H A
A A A M O X
P T E E N Z
Q N L A M B
E G Q J P A
R A B B I T

Short ĕ has the sound of the **e** in the words **yes**, **less** and **guess**. **Yes**, **less** and **guess** are also rhyming words because they end with the same sound. Look at each pair of **short ĕ** pictures below. If the names of the pictures rhyme, put a check mark (✓) on the line next to the pair.

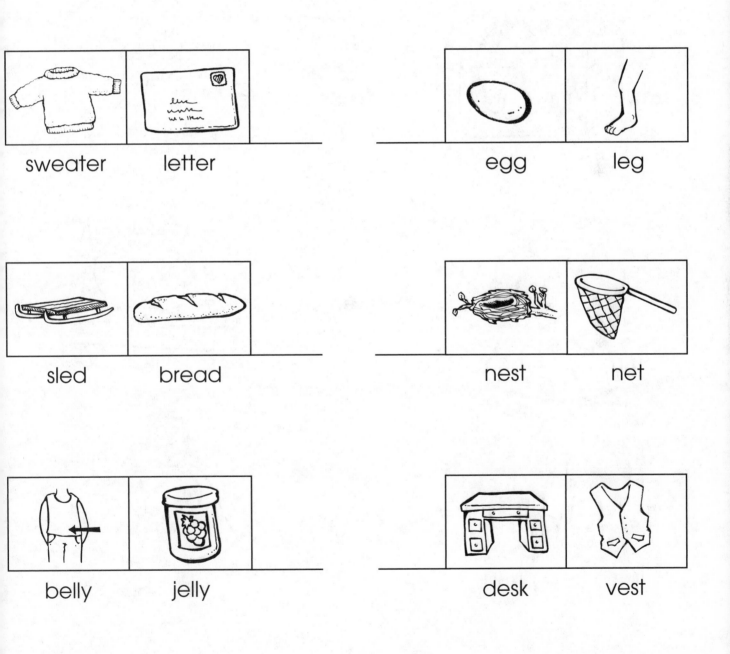

sweater   letter

egg   leg

sled   bread

nest   net

belly   jelly

desk   vest

Some words have more than one meaning. Say each **short ĕ** word below. Then, find the two pictures that show what that word means. Draw lines from both pictures to the **short ĕ** word.

dress

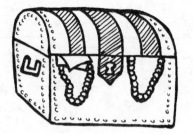

pen

chest

The crossword puzzle on this page has **short ĕ** words. Use the numbered clues to complete the puzzle. The first one is done for you.

Across

2. something a spider builds
5. a spotted cat
6. more than one man

Down

1. a tool for writing
3. they cover a bird's body
4. a place to sleep

Short ĭ

Short ĭ Bingo

Short ĭ has the sound of the i in the words **bingo** and **win**. Ask an adult to help you play a game of **short ĭ** bingo. Here is what you will need to make the game. Get everything together before you begin to play.

Now, follow these directions in order.

1. With a pair of scissors, cut out nine small squares of paper.

2. Write one word on each square. Use these words: **nickel**, **pig**, **ring**, **hill**, **zip**, **mitt**, **milk**, **dig**, and **pickle**.

3. Put the squares of paper inside a paper bag.

4. Have your adult friend pull one square at a time from the bag and read the word on it to you.

5. Find the picture that shows what the word means on the bingo card on the next page. Put a coin over that picture.

6. Continue this way until one row has three coins on it. Rows on your bingo card can either go across (→) or down (↓).

7. When you have a row with three coins, yell the word BINGO! You have won the game.

BINGO CARD

After you have won, you can use your bingo card to play again and again!

Short ĭ

The **Short Ĭ** Bridge is for animals whose names make the **short ĭ** sound. Which animals do not belong on this bridge? Draw an **X** on any animal whose name has a different vowel sound.

chimp

pig

cricket

fish

spider

lizard

Now, color all the animals that have **short ĭ** names.

dinosaur

chipmunk

chicken

giraffe

tiger

hippo

Short ŏ

Short ŏ has the sound of the **o** in the words **dog** and **knock**. Look at the pictures below. Then, say each picture's name out loud. Draw a line through any picture with a different vowel sound.

Oscar is filling a box with things whose names have the **short ŏ** sound. Help him decide which ones to put in the box. Draw a square around each **short ŏ** picture. Circle each picture whose name has a different sound.

Short ŭ

Short ŭ has the sound of the **u** in the name **Rusty** and the word **puzzle**. Rusty the juggler is juggling balls with **short ŭ** words on them! Find and circle the words in the puzzle. Words can go either across (→) or down (↓).

P	U	Z	Z	L	E	X	
U	A	B	R	U	S	H	
M	E	O	F	A	B	S	
P	T	D	U	G	U	M	
K	A	R	N	E	Z	Q	
A	B	U	L	Y	Z	M	
N	U	M	B	E	R	F	
I	S	T	R	U	C	K	

Use the code box below to help you read the **short ŭ** story. First, look at the number under each line below. Then, find the letter that goes with that number in the code box. Write that letter on the line. Fill in all the letters to complete the story. When you are finished, read the story out loud.

CODE

1 = A	4 = D	7 = I	10 = R
2 = B	5 = E	8 = K	11 = S
3 = C	6 = H	9 = N	12 = U
	13 = T		

___ ___ ___   ___ ___ ___   ___ ___ ___
13   6   5   3   12   2   1   9   4

___ ___ ___   ___ ___ ___ ___ ___   ___ ___ ___
13   6   5   11   8   12   9   8   3   12   13

___ ___ ___ ___ ___ ___   ___ ___
2   12   13   13   5   10   7   9

___ ___ ___   ___ ___ ___ .
13   6   5   11   12   9

Short Vowel Review

Jack is going on a trip. He is packing only short vowel clothes. Help Jack figure out what to pack. Use crayons to color all the clothes that have **short vowel** names.

Fancy Nancy is a short vowel robot. The names of the parts it took to put her together are listed below. Say the name of each part. Then, write the **short vowel** sound you hear next to each part.

head _____

lips _____

chin _____

neck _____

chest _____

tummy _____

wrist _____

hand _____

thumb _____

hip _____

leg _____

calf _____

finger _____

Short and Long Vowel Review

The animals need to board the ark in pairs. A **pair** is two things that go together. Put the animals in pairs by their vowel sounds: **short ă** with **long ā**, **short ĕ** with **long ē**, **short ĭ** with **long ī**, and so on. Draw lines to connect the animals in each pair.

The name of a color is written on each crayon below. Say each color's name and listen for the vowel sounds. Some of the colors may have more than one vowel sound. On the line under each crayon, write all the **vowel sounds** you hear. Then, use your crayons to color each crayon picture its correct color.

Around the outside of the circle below are numbers. Inside the circle are vowel sounds. Say each number out loud. Then, find the vowel sound of the number's name inside the circle. Draw a line from the number to the vowel sound.

An **r blend** is a sound made by adding **r** after another consonant. Combine each set of consonants below, then write the **r blend** you make in the box. Then, draw a line connecting each **r blend** with the picture with that sound.

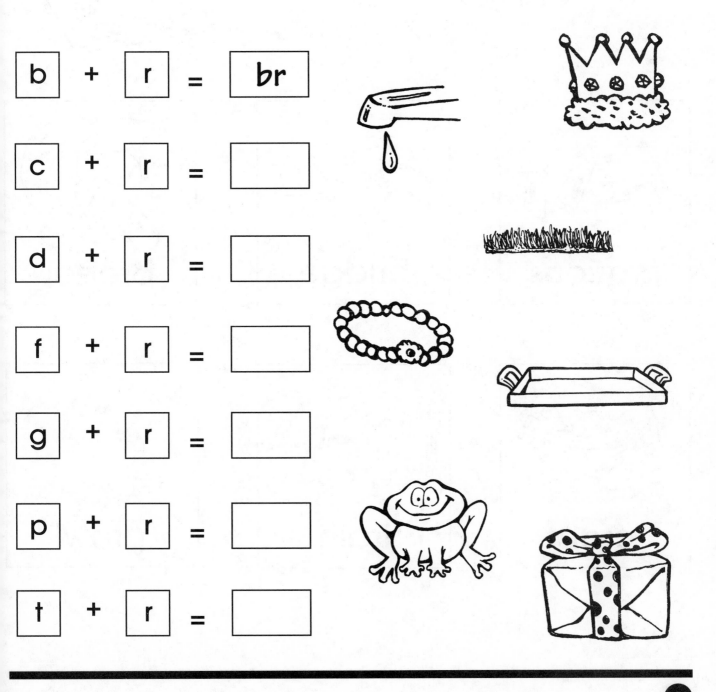

b	+	r	=	br
c	+	r	=	
d	+	r	=	
f	+	r	=	
g	+	r	=	
p	+	r	=	
t	+	r	=	

r Consonant Blends

Drew is using his crayons to draw **r blend** words. Look at his pictures below and say each word. Circle the **r blend** in it. Then, use your crayons to color each picture that Drew drew.

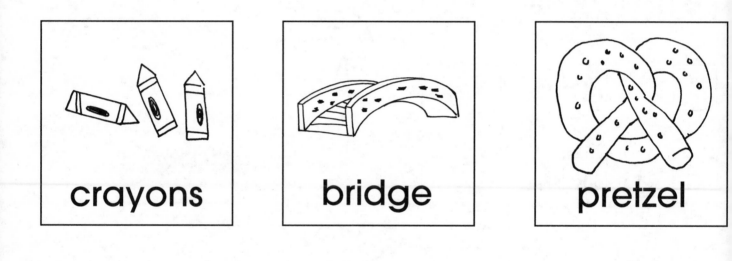

crayons

bridge

pretzel

crab

train

growl

Look at each word inside the block below. Draw a line under the **l** and the letter before it. Now, look at all the words again. Find a row of words that has the same **l blend**. Use a crayon to color in that row. The row can go across (→), down (↓) or diagonally (↙↘).

flag	climb	blimp	globe
plate	flame	sleep	glad
plus	clap	floor	black
plant	blue	fly	flip

Flo is cleaning out her **l blend** closet. Help her by drawing an **X** on any picture whose name does not contain an **l blend**. Then, say the names of the rest of the pictures. Write each two-letter blend on one of the lines on the closet door.

Use the code box below to complete the **s blend** words. Look at the number under each line. Then, write the corresponding **s blend** on the line. When you are done, read each word out loud.

CODE

1 = sk   5 = sp
2 = sl   6 = st
3 = sm   7 = sw
4 = sn

___ i
1

___ in
5

___ op
6

___ ow
4

___ ed
2

___ ing
7

___ ide
2

___ ar
6

___ ile
3

___ im
7

___ in
1

___ ap
4

s Consonant Blends

Some **s blends** contain three letters instead of two. Circle the
s blend in each word in the box. Then, find and circle the words in
the puzzle below. Words can go across (→) or down (↓).

scream	stretch	splash	sprout
strike	spray	scrub	splits

```
S T R I K E L U
C S C R U B E S
R Q S P R O U T
E S P R A Y N R
A P L O L S T E
M L I R S C R T
N S T R H O S C
X A S P L A S H
```

Riley the Rhyming Rabbit loves to make up rhymes. Help him change the blend in each word on the left to make a different word that rhymes. First, read the word on the left. Then, look at the three choices of blends on the right. Draw a box around each blend that would make a word that rhymes. Say each new word real loud.

fry	**sk**	**sw**	**fl**
slow	**sn**	**gr**	**cr**
stop	**dr**	**bl**	**cr**
play	**cl**	**st**	**spr**
dream	**scr**	**str**	**gr**
swing	**spr**	**str**	**br**
splash	**tr**	**sn**	**cr**
drip	**fl**	**tr**	**sl**

Digraphs

The **th digraph** sounds like the **th** in the words **thunder** and **thorn**. Say the names of all the numbers in the box below. Whenever you say a number word that has a **th digraph**, use your favorite color crayon to color in that square.

14	26	3
50	33	10
9	66	13
30	37	44

An **h digraph** is a sound made by adding the letter **h** after another consonant. Say **wish**. The sound at the end of the word is the **sh digraph** sound. Now, say **cheese**. The sound at the beginning is the **ch digraph** sound. To play this game, look for the **h digraphs** in the picture below. Circle each picture which has an **sh** sound. Draw a box around each picture which has a **ch** sound.

Blends and Digraphs Review

Today's menu is filled with foods whose names have consonant blends and digraphs. Look at the words on the menu the chef is holding. Then, circle those words in the puzzle. Words can go across (→) or down (↓).

MENU

cheese
grapes
bread
fish

chicken
strawberries
peaches
pretzels

```
C  H  I  C  K  E  N  R  S
A  X  D  H  M  V  F  M  T
R  T  G  E  W  I  X  S  R
K  B  R  E  A  D  C  Q  A
N  I  A  S  T  P  O  F  W
O  B  P  E  R  J  S  I  B
P  R  E  T  Z  E  L  S  E
Y  I  S  Q  E  R  J  H  R
Q  P  E  A  C  H  E  S  R
E  Z  N  X  E  W  E  R  I
D  C  H  E  R  R  I  S  E
R  O  K  H  C  L  Z  Y  S
```

Sentence Sense

Sentences tell you about someone or something. Read the sentences below. Then, look at the pictures. Draw a line from each picture to the sentence that describes it.

The cat is on the rug.

The dog has a slipper.

It is raining.

A boat is in the water.

A bird is flying.

A cup is on the table.

The bike is broken.

The two balls are alike.

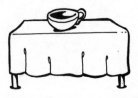

Read the two sentences below.

Mary chased the cat.

The cat chased Mary.

The order of words affects the meaning of a sentence. In the first sentence, Mary does the chasing. In the second sentence, the cat does the chasing!

Circle the sentences below that describe the pictures.

The book is on the table.

The table is on the book.

A dog is behind a tree.

A tree is behind a dog.

A bird sees a worm.

A worm sees a bird.

The bug is on the mat.

The mat is on the bug.

Sentence Sense

Help Stanley finish the sentences so they make sense. Use the words in the word box.

two hot dogs	a funny book
barked loudly	a big truck
flew up high	a new pencil

Jan read _____.

The dog _____.

Pat ate _____.

I wrote with _____.

The man drove _____.

A little bird _____.

The words in the sentences below are all mixed up. Write the words in the correct order on the lines.

went   Jack   the   to   zoo.

_____

some   saw   He   monkeys.

_____

a   in   They   tree.   were

_____

playing.   They   were

_____

to   Jack   waved   them.

_____

Capital Letters—First Word in a Sentence

When writing sentences,
don't forget Elmer
Elephant's rule.

Every sentence begins
with a capital letter.

Read the sentences. Circle each word that needs a capital letter.
Write the words correctly on the lines.

colorful flags waved in the air. _____

inside a tent sat many people. _____

red balloons bobbed up and down. _____

clowns did funny tricks. _____

up on a chair jumped a monkey. _____

six horses trotted in a circle. _____

Where does Elmer work? To find out, write each capital letter in
order on the lines below.

Elmer works at a ___ ___ ___ ___ ___ ___.

People's names begin with capital letters. Read the sentences below. Write the names correctly on the lines.

Hello!
My name is brad.

Hello!
My name is carla.

Hello!
My name is meg.

Hello!
My name is dave.

Hello!
My name is kirk.

Hello!
My name is lisa.

Capital Letters—Days of the Week

The names of the days of the week begin with capital letters. Read the sentences below. Circle the names of the days. Write them correctly on the lines.

Sunday
Monday

Tuesday
Wednesday
Thursday

Friday
Saturday

I saw Ben on monday. _____

Today is saturday. _____

We went camping on friday. _____

Tomorrow is sunday. _____

Kate was ill on wednesday. _____

Tony helped me on thursday. _____

Chris played soccer on tuesday. _____

The months of the year begin with capital letters.

January	May	September
February	June	October
March	July	November
April	August	December

Write the missing letters to complete the names of the months below. Use the letters on the balloons. Cross out each letter as you use it.

___ebruary   ___ctober

___uly   ___pril

___ay   ___anuary

___ecember   ___eptember

___ugust   ___une

___arch   ___ovember

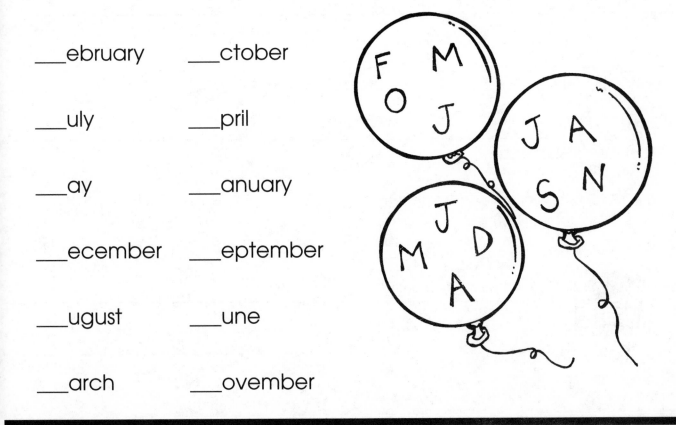

Capital Letters—Holidays

The names of holidays begin with
capital letters. Here are the names
of some holidays.

Valentine's Day	Fourth of July	Thanksgiving
Easter	Halloween	Christmas

Write the names of the holidays beside the matching pictures.
Don't forget to use capital letters!

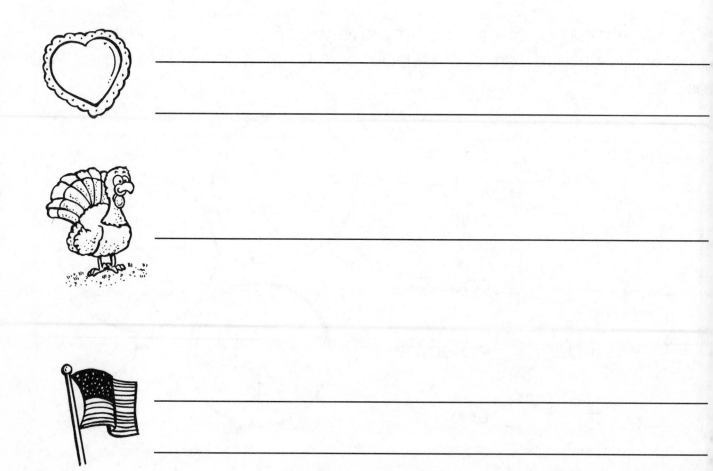

Who is in the picture? To find out, use brown to color the spaces that have words needing capital letters.

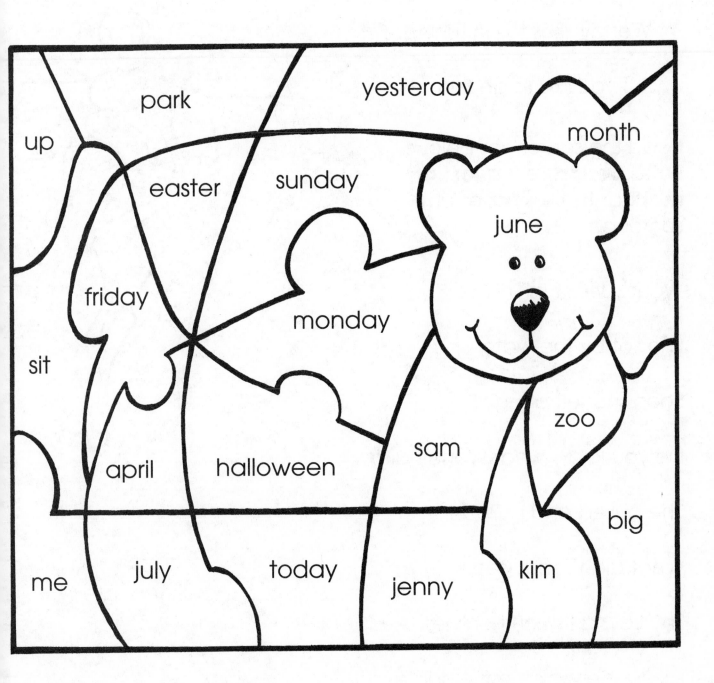

Periods and Question Marks

Sentences that tell something end with a **period** (**.**). Sentences that ask something end with a **question mark** (**?**). Look at these two examples.

Wendy likes to go fishing.

Do you like to go fishing?

Read the sentences below. Put a **period** or a **question mark** at the end of each sentence.

Wendy went fishing

She sat by the water

Soon she felt a tug

Do you know what Wendy did

She pulled and pulled

What did Wendy see

She saw a fish on her line

Later, she took the fish home

Read each sentence below. Add a **period** at the end if the sentence tells something. Add a **question mark** if the sentence asks something.

Farmer Bill is outside

What is he doing

He is feeding the animals

He gives the chicks some corn

Are the horses hungry

The horses want to eat some hay

What will Farmer Bill do next

He will go to the store

Do you think Farmer Bill is busy

Are you as busy as Farmer Bill

Punctuation Review

Can you help Terry Turtle with his work? Write each sentence correctly. Use **capital letters**. Put in **periods** and **question marks**.

today is friday

_____

do you know why

_____

my friend bert is coming

_____

we are going to the pond

_____

where do you like to go

_____

Some words name only one person or thing (**ball**). Other words name more than one (**balls**).

Words that name more than one person or thing are called **plurals**. You often make plurals by adding **s** to the end of a word.

Change the words below to **plurals**.

jet _____

duck _____

doll _____

drum _____

car _____

top _____

game _____

horn _____

Circle the word that describes each picture.

frog
frogs

turtle
turtles

owl
owls

ant
ants

snake
snakes

tree
trees

pond
ponds

bear
bears

A **plural** is a word that means more than one person or thing. You can add **s** or **es** to the end of a word to make a plural.

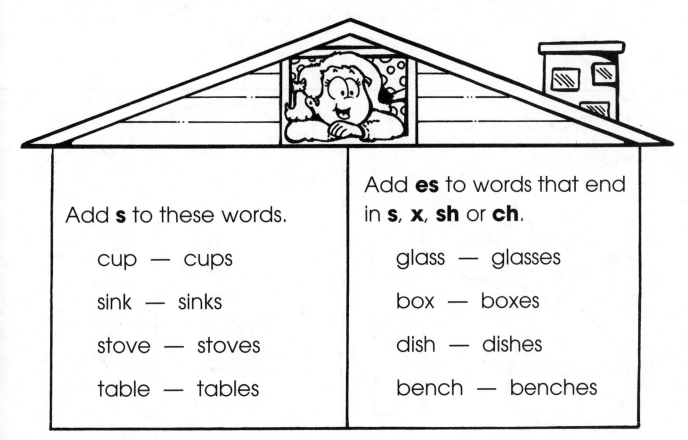

Add **s** to these words.

cup — cups

sink — sinks

stove — stoves

table — tables

Add **es** to words that end in **s**, **x**, **sh** or **ch**.

glass — glasses

box — boxes

dish — dishes

bench — benches

Write the **plurals** of these words.

house _____

bush _____

dress _____

lamp _____

bus _____

fox _____

rug _____

peach _____

Plurals Review

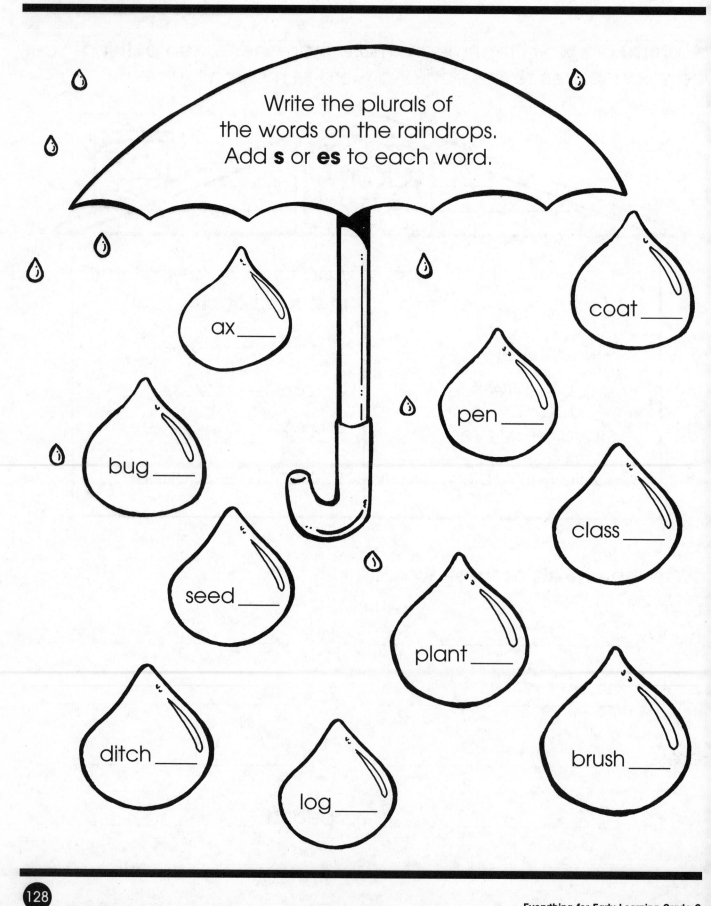

Write the plurals of
the words on the raindrops.
Add **s** or **es** to each word.

ax____

coat____

pen____

bug____

class____

seed____

plant____

ditch____

log____

brush____

Contractions are words that are made from two words with one or more letters left out. A mark called an **apostrophe** (') is used in place of the missing letters.

do not

don't

Find the contraction for the word pair in each boat. Draw a line from the boat to the correct fish.

are not

aren't

wasn't

did not

was not

didn't

doesn't

does not

cannot

can't

haven't

have not

Contractions

Write the **contraction** for the words on each ice-cream cone. Use the words that are on the carton.

it's	that's
he's	I'm
she's	you're
we're	they're

he is

it is

you are

we are

she is

I am

that is

they are

Read each sentence. Write the **contraction** for the two words that are below each line. Use the words that are on the kite.

I'll
she'll
we'll   he'll
they'll
it'll

_____ meet Paul at the park.
I will

I hope _____ be windy.
it will

Paul said _____ bring his kite.
he will

His mom said _____ help us.
she will

I think _____ be there soon.
they will

Later, _____ go get a snack.
we will

Contractions

Write the **contraction** for each pair of words. Use the words on the stars to help you.

do not _____

is not _____

you are _____

she will _____

they will _____

we are _____

I am _____

he is _____

cannot _____

they are _____

isn't

don't

can't

I'm

he's

we're

you're

they're

she'll

they'll

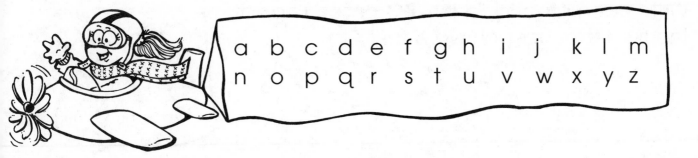

a b c d e f g h i j k l m
n o p q r s t u v w x y z

Write the letter that comes **after** each letter.

a, _____   g, _____   j, _____   m, _____   p, _____

d, _____   s, _____   o, _____   w, _____   e, _____

Write the letter that comes **before** each letter.

_____, m   _____, x   _____, c   _____, o   _____, k

_____, v   _____, z   _____, f   _____, y   _____, s

Try to solve this riddle!

What bird is always sad?

To find the answer, write the
letter that comes **after** each
letter shown below.

‾‾ ‾‾ ‾‾   ‾‾ ‾‾ ‾‾ ‾‾ ‾‾ ‾‾ ‾‾ ‾‾
 s g d   a k t d a h q c

ABC Order

Write each grocery list in **ABC order**. Look at the first letter of each word for help.

apple
bread
cheese

milk
eggs
butter

_____

_____

_____

ham
grapes
peas

_____

_____

_____

pie
juice
corn

_____

_____

_____

beans
soup
fish

_____

_____

_____

A **compound word** is a word that is made up of two smaller words. Look at the words below the pictures. Put the words together to make **compound words**. Write the new words on the lines.

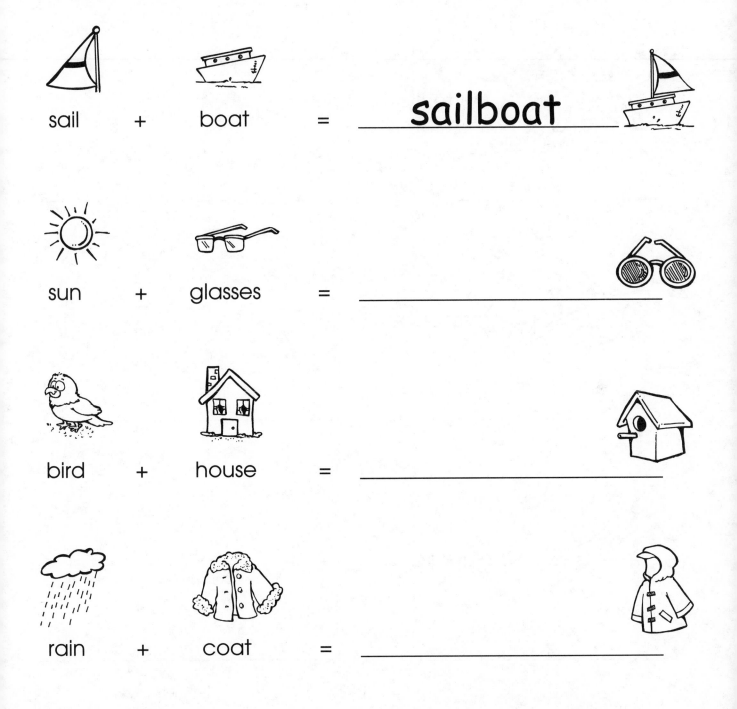

sail   +   boat   =   sailboat

sun   +   glasses   = _____

bird   +   house   = _____

rain   +   coat   = _____

Compound Words

Can you find the two words that make up each animal's name?
Write them on the lines.

 butterfly

_____   _____

 grasshopper

_____   _____

bluebird

_____   _____

Write the **compound word** that matches each description. Use the words in the box.

gumdrop   peanut   cupcake

milkshake   popcorn   strawberry

This fruit is red. _____

This grows inside a shell. _____

This snack is made from corn. _____

This drink is sweet and cool. _____

This is a small candy. _____

This is baked in an oven. _____

Compound Words Review

Find the hidden picture. Color each space that has a compound word **orange**. Color the other spaces **blue**.

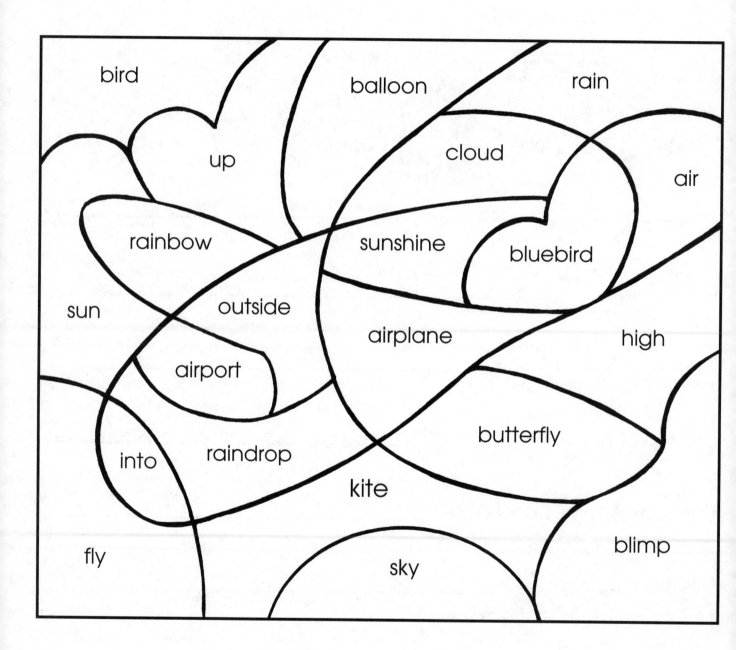

Action words tell what a person or a thing can do.

Examples:

The frog **hops**.   The frogs **hop**.

An action word usually ends in **s** when it tells about only one person or thing. An action word usually does not end in **s** when it tells about more than one person or thing.

Circle the correct **action word** for each sentence.

The boy **read**, **reads**.

The girl **eat**, **eats**.

The lion **roar**, **roars**.

The whale **swim**, **swims**.

The baby **play**, **plays**.

The phone **ring**, **rings**.

The books **fall**, **falls**.

Verb Forms

Some **action words** tell about something that has already happened.

Example: Yesterday I **painted** a picture.

You add **ed** to most action words to tell about something that has happened in the past.

Add **ed** to these words.

jump _____   plant _____   wash _____

walk _____   cook _____   bark _____

Use your new words to complete these sentences.

Last night, our dog _____ loudly.

Yesterday, I _____ to school.

My mom _____ flowers on Sunday.

A cat _____ down from the fence.

My dad _____ dinner two days ago.

We _____ the dishes this morning.

Some **action words** tell about something that is happening now. These words usually have **ing** at the end.

Examples: My family is **eating**.

We are **enjoying** a picnic.

Add **ing** to these words.

play _____   watch _____   buy _____

talk _____   open _____   read _____

Use your new words to complete these sentences.

The teacher is _____ a story.

Sandy is _____ the piano quietly.

We are _____ a new house.

The boy is _____ his gift.

The children are _____ a movie.

I am _____ to my new friend.

Word Usage

When you talk about one person or thing, use **is**. When you talk about more than one person or thing, use **are**.

Examples:

The boat **is** in the water.

The boats **are** in the water.

Write **is** or **are** on the blank lines.

The boy and girl _____ on a boat.

The boat _____ big and safe.

The children _____ with their friend.

A whale _____ in the water.

The children _____ excited.

The girl _____ waving hello.

Which flowers have the words that complete the sentences correctly? Color them.

Scott is ____ some flowers.

pick — picking

Bev ____ her bike every day.

ride — rides

We ____ baseball last week.

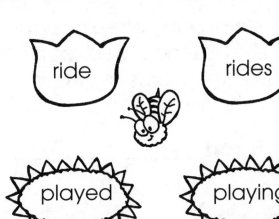

played — playing

The girls are ____ for bugs.

looks — looking

They are ____ to the park.

walked — walking

The boys ____ on the bars.

hang — hangs

Synonyms

Synonyms are words that
have the same, or almost
the same, meaning. For
example, **big** and **large**
are synonyms. You can replace
a word in a sentence with its synonym.

big   large

Choose **synonyms** to replace the words
in bold. Look at the pieces of paper for
clues. Write the words on the lines.

closed

The boy is **sad**. _____

unhappy

The door is **shut**. _____

stone

An ant is **little**. _____

yelled

The flowers are **pretty**. _____

leap

This **rock** is smooth. _____

Kangaroos can **jump** in the air. _____

lovely

Leslie **shouted** across the room. _____

small

Antonyms are words that have opposite meanings. For example, the words **up** and **down** are antonyms.

Write the **antonyms** of the words in bold in the sentences below. Use the words in the box to help you.

dry	last	low	tall
cold	slowly	small	hard

We have a **big** garden. _____

It is a **hot** day. _____

This plant is **short**. _____

The grass is **wet**. _____

The ground is **soft**. _____

Some bugs move **quickly**. _____

The birds are flying **high**. _____

Let's pick these flowers **first**. _____

Homophones

Homophones are words that sound the same but have different meanings.

Examples: I ate a **pear**.

I have a **pair** of shoes.

Pear and **pair** are homophones.

Match the **homophones**. Write the words from the tree on the lines below.

sea

rode   blew

hear   know

eye

I   _____

see   _____

blue   _____

road   _____

here   _____

no   _____

Try to solve these puzzles. Read the clues and use the words in the box. The words go down (↓) then across (→).

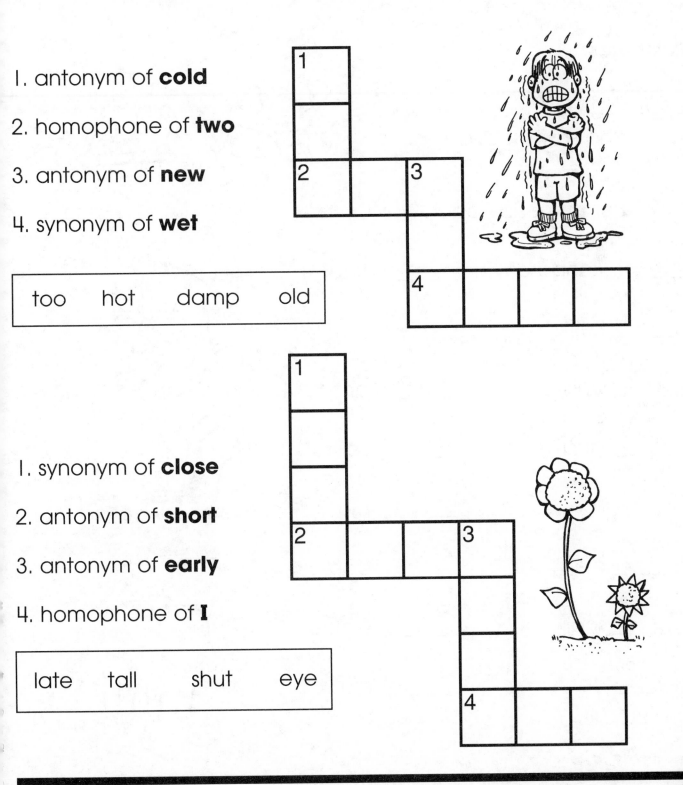

1. antonym of **cold**

2. homophone of **two**

3. antonym of **new**

4. synonym of **wet**

| too | hot | damp | old |

1. synonym of **close**

2. antonym of **short**

3. antonym of **early**

4. homophone of **I**

| late | tall | shut | eye |

Word Usage

When you talk about a person or a thing, use **a** if the next word begins with a consonant sound. Use **an** if the next word begins with a vowel sound.

Examples:

Kevin saw **a** turtle.

Marsha saw **an** owl.

Write **a** or **an** beside each word.

_____ kangaroo   _____ tiger

_____ ostrich   _____ cat

_____ frog   _____ ant

_____ goat   _____ zebra

_____ lion   _____ pig

_____ elephant   _____ dog

_____ snail   _____ whale

_____ bat   _____ skunk

Describing words can tell how a person, a place or a thing looks.

Example:

Emma found a coin.

Emma found a **shiny** coin.

The word **shiny** describes how the coin looks.

Circle the **describing word** in each sentence. Then, draw a line from the word to the correct picture.

The baby has a striped ball.

The clown has a pointed hat.

Vic found a long rope.

A thick book is on the table.

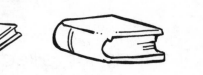

Describing Words

Describing words can also tell about an action.

Examples:

The turtle moved **slowly**.

The rabbit moved **quickly**.

The word **slowly** describes how the turtle moved. The word **quickly** describes how the rabbit moved.

Write a word to describe each action below. Choose a word from the box, or use a word of your own.

Sidney played the piano _____.

The child sang _____.

The horse ran _____.

The snow fell _____.

The man drove _____.

The teacher talked _____.

loudly
softly
quickly
slowly
sadly
happily

Describing words can also help make sentences more interesting.

Example:

The bear is climbing the tree.

The **huge** bear is climbing the tree **carefully**.

The words **huge** and **carefully** help "paint a picture" in your mind about what is happening.

Make the sentences below more interesting by adding **describing words**.

The _____ fish swam in the sea.

The _____ man sat down.

The girl danced _____ across the stage.

The birds chirped _____ in the tree.

The _____ animal came near me.

The _____ student waved _____.

Word Usage

Here's Sue. She is a **good** skater. She skates **well**.

When you describe a person, a place or a thing, use **good**. When you describe how something is done, use **well**.

Circle **good** or **well** in each sentence.

Andrew is a **good**, **well** singer.

Wanda dances **good**, **well**.

Antonio writes stories **good**, **well**.

Tim is a **good**, **well** reader.

Carmen is a **good**, **well** cook.

Helen paints **good**, **well**.

Doug adds numbers **good**, **well**.

Help the coach get to the castle. Complete each sentence on the path with the correct word.

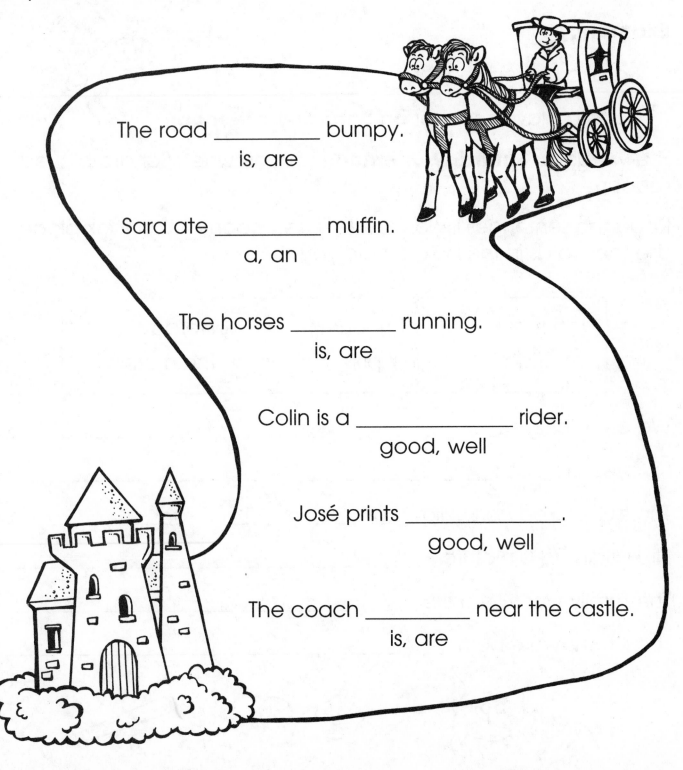

The road _____ bumpy.
is, are

Sara ate _____ muffin.
a, an

The horses _____ running.
is, are

Colin is a _____ rider.
good, well

José prints _____.
good, well

The coach _____ near the castle.
is, are

Expanding Sentences

You can make sentences more interesting by telling **when** something happened.

Example:

Sandra played soccer.

Sandra played soccer **on Saturday afternoon**.

The words **on Saturday afternoon** tell you when Sandra played soccer.

Read the sentences below. Write when each action took place. Use the words in the box to help you.

last week	at noon	yesterday
on Friday	in April	in the morning

We ate muffins _____.

I played baseball _____.

The bus picked up Emilio _____.

Nikki painted a picture _____.

The family went on a trip _____.

The kittens were born _____.

You can make sentences more interesting by using **colorful words**.

Example:

Fred walked into the room.

Fred **tiptoed** into the room.

The second sentence gives you a better idea of how Fred went into the room. The word **tiptoed** "paints a picture" in your mind.

Read the sentences below. Write a **colorful word** for each bold word. Choose words from the box.

sipped	soared	wailed
gobbled	whispered	crawled

The girl **drank** the milk. _____

Some ants **moved** along the wall. _____

The wolf **ate** the food. _____

The baby **cried** at the store. _____

A bird **flew** above me. _____

The boy **talked** to his friend. _____

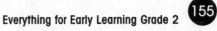

Language Review

Read the sentences below. For each sentence, circle the word that describes a person, a place or a thing.

The scared kitten hid.

We went into a dark cave.

The new park has a slide.

A shiny button is on the floor.

Read the sentences below. For each sentence, circle the word that describes an action.

Clara printed neatly.

A car was honking loudly.

Marco read quietly.

The children ran quickly.

Write a sentence to describe each picture. Here are some questions that can help you decide what to write. Who is in the picture? What is happening? Where is it happening? When is it happening? You may use the words below to help you.

bee

bear

running

_____

_____

_____

car

clown

riding

_____

_____

_____

_____

Sentence Order

When you write a story, put the sentences in **order** so the story makes sense.

Example: Eve got out the paints.

She painted a picture.

Eve hung the picture on the wall.

Read the sentences below. Write them in **order** so that they tell a story.

Sam ate the peas.

Sam washed the peas.

He cooked the peas.

_____

_____

_____

The seeds grew into plants.

Jasmine dug a hole.

She put seeds in the hole.

_____

_____

_____

Did you know that you are a very special person? There is no one who is just like you! Draw a picture of yourself in the frame. Then, write at least three sentences about yourself on the lines below.

_____

_____

_____

_____

_____

_____

_____

Writing a Story

Write a story about three things you did today. Write what you did first. Then, write what you did next. Finally, write what you did last.

MATH

Size and Shape Comparisons

When you **compare** objects, you look to see how they are the same or how they are different.

Pug and Gogg are the same size.

Stump and James are not the same size. Stump is **smaller**, and James is **bigger**.

Pug   Gogg   Stump   James

In each box, two monsters are the **same** size. Circle them.

Two pictures in each box are the **same** size and shape.
Draw a circle around the ones that are the same.

These prints have the
same shape.

These have a
different shape.

Size and Shape Comparisons

Circle the **biggest** picture in each box.

Trace the smallest picture in the boxes below. Then, draw the other two sizes on your own. The first one is done for you.

Smallest   **Bigger**   **Biggest**

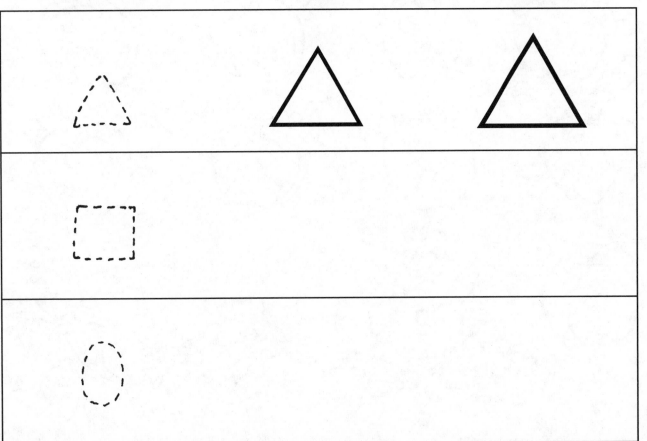

Counting 1 to 10

Help the monsters below line up in the correct order. The first monster is 1. The last monster is 10. Fill in each pumpkin with the correct number, so the other monsters know where to stand in line.

The monsters are having a good time! They love Halloween parties.

How many monsters have caramel apples? _____

How many monsters are playing "Pin the Tail on the Black

Cat"? _____

Draw a circle around each monster with a trick-or-treat

bag. _____

How many monsters are at the party? _____

Matching Like Objects

Monsters love to dance! Everyone is wearing special dancing shoes.

Help the monsters on the left find their partners on the right. Draw a line to connect the partners who are wearing the same kinds of shoes.

How many pairs of partners are at the dance? _____

Draw a circle around the monster without a partner.

Mr. Masher, who wears glasses, is looking for his child. His child has:

a pointed hat
a belt
six fingers
a bandaged knee
a watch
an untied shoe
a crooked nose

How many monsters

are dancing? _____

How many pairs are dancing? _____

How many monsters wear a belt? _____

How many monsters have a bandaged knee? _____

How many monsters have a crooked nose? _____

Circle Mr. Masher's child.

More Than

Help Monty decide which branch has more bananas on it. One has 7 bananas on it. The other has 5.

7 is **more than** **5**

Sometimes, we write **more than** with a **symbol** that looks like this: **>**. On the line below, trace the math symbol that means **more than**.

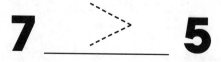

Monty and his friend Manuel have eaten a lot of bananas! Count the banana peels. Then, write the numbers on the lines below.

Who has eaten **more** bananas? _____

_____ is **more than** _____

Write in the missing math symbol on the line.

7 _____ 4

Less Than

Henrietta Hen has fewer eggs in one basket than in another. Point to the basket that holds **less**.

6 is **less than** **7**

Sometimes, we write **less than** using the symbol: **<**.
On the line below, write the math symbol that means **less than**.

6 _____ **7**

Now, count the
decorated eggs.
Then, fill in the numbers
and math symbol to
the right!

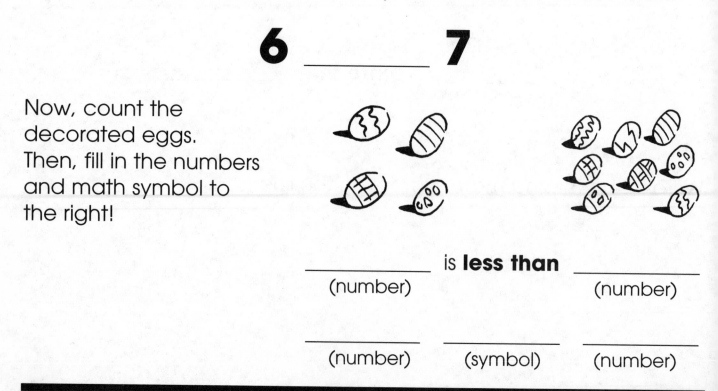

_____ is **less than** _____
(number)   (number)

_____ _____ _____
(number)   (symbol)   (number)

Blue Sky, a Navajo girl, is watching some number clouds in the sky! For each pair of numbers, draw a circle around the number that is **more**.

Blue Sky's brother, Falling Star, is watching the number clouds, too. In each pair, circle the number that is **less**.

Look at each tray of chocolate chip cookies. Count the number of chocolate chips each cookie on the trays has. Then, circle the cookie next to each tray that has the same number of chocolate chips as the ones on the tray.

Color the cookie which has the **most** chocolate chips **green**.
Color the cookie which has the **fewest** chocolate chips **blue**.

Circle the row in the rug that has **more** feathers in it.
How many **more** feathers does this row have? _____

Top Row

Bottom Row

Now, cross out the row that has **fewer**. How many **fewer** does it have? _____

How many feathers would you need to add to this row to make it **equal to** (the same as) the other row? _____

When you put numbers and symbols together to figure out a problem, you are writing an equation. Finish the equation.

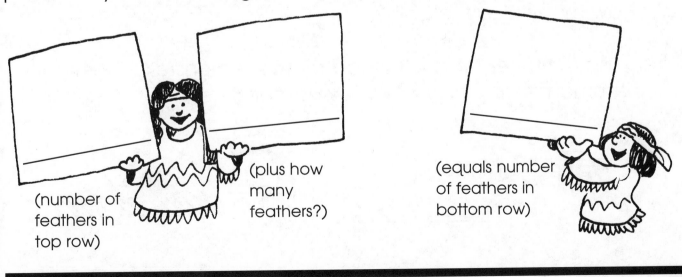

(number of feathers in top row)

(plus how many feathers?)

(equals number of feathers in bottom row)

More/Less

The monsters are waiting for their band instruments to arrive. There are tubas, flutes, trumpets and bells. Can you figure out how many monsters play each of the instruments? Use the clues below to answer each question.

- More than 5 but less than 7 monsters play the trumpet.
  How many play the trumpet? _____
- Less than 4 but more than 2 monsters play the flute.
  How many play the flute? _____
- More than 1 but less than 3 monsters play the tuba.
  How many play the tuba? _____
- More than 3 but less than 5 monsters play the bells.
  How many play the bells? _____

Circle the instrument that is played by **more** monsters. Cross out the instrument that is played by **fewer** monsters.

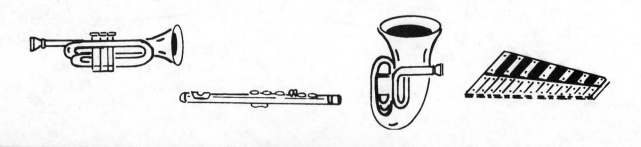

The monster boys and girls from Slimepit Elementary School have been on a field trip to the Green Swamp. Now, it is time to go home. Gus, the bus driver, needs to count all 20 passengers. He is marking off 1 square on his chart for each passenger as he or she boards the bus. Help Gus by filling in the missing numbers on his chart. Then, count the monsters in line. Is everybody there?

More/Less

The bus is rolling back toward Slimepit Elementary. What are the monster children doing to pass the time as they travel?

Are **more** monsters reading or listening to music? _____

Are **fewer** monsters sleeping or reading? _____

Mikey Monster is making a calendar for the month of May. He wants to make sure that he remembers to celebrate his birthday! Help him fill in the missing numbers on his calendar. Use these clues to figure out the date of Mikey's birthday.

Use these clues to figure out the date of Mikey's birthday.

- It is a number greater than 5.
- It ends with a zero.
- It does not fall on a Saturday.
- It is a number less than 24.

Draw a star on the calendar to mark Mikey's birthday.

Counting by 2's

All these monsters have come to the tennis court to play in a tournament. How many are there?

_2_   ___   ___   ___   ___

Instead of counting the monsters in the usual way, count by 2's. There are 2 monsters in the first pair, so put a 2 on the line beneath them. 2 more monsters make 4. Now, fill in the rest of the blanks.

The Frundell family is a very unusual monster family. They are known as the "Fearsome Frundells" because each member of the family has 5 frightening horns growing out of his or her head. How many horns do the Fearsome Frundells have altogether?

We don't have to count the horns one by one to find out! We can count by 5's.

5   10   ____   ____   ____

Each monster has 5 horns, so we can begin with the number 5. 5 plus 5 more is 10, so put a 10 on the next line. 10 and 5 more equal what number? Write it under the third monster. Finish the rest of the row.

Addition

Putting numbers together is called **addition**. When you **add** two numbers together, you get a **total**, or **sum**. The symbol used for addition is called a **plus sign** (**+**). The symbol used for a total is an **equal sign** (**=**).

Follow the instructions below to create and solve the addition problems.

I pony is eating hay.	Draw I more pony in this box.	Write the total number of ponies.

I lamb is jumping.	Draw 2 more lambs in this box.	Write the total number of lambs.

The Barton family is having a picnic. But the ants have carried away their food. Use an addition equation to find out how many ants took food. The first one is done for you.

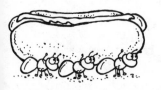

How many ants carried away fruit?

_____1_____ + _____2_____ = _____3_____

(one plus two equals three)

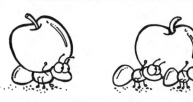

How many ants carried away vegetables?

_____ + _____ = _____

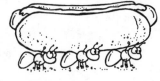

How many ants carried away hot dogs?

_____ + _____ = _____

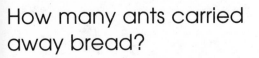

How many ants carried away bread?

_____ + _____ = _____

Addition

Add up the dots on the domino pieces below. Write the total on the line below each piece.

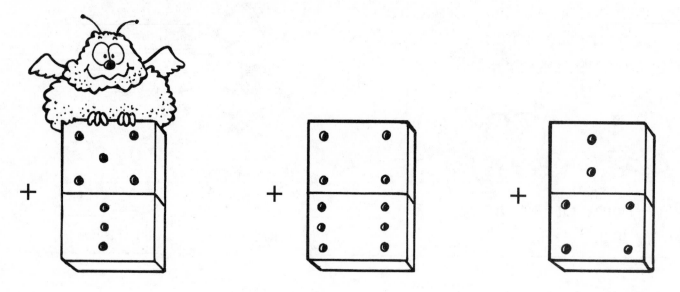

+ _____   + _____   + _____

Now, draw the missing dots on each domino. Make sure the total number of dots adds up to the total on the line beneath each domino.

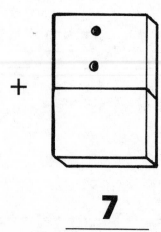   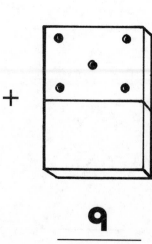   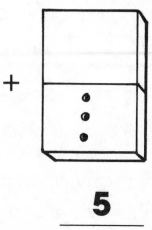

+ **7** _____   + **9** _____   + **5** _____

The geese are taking a stroll in the park. Use crayons to color 2 geese red, 3 geese green, 4 geese blue and 5 geese yellow.

Complete the addition equations to show how many geese of each color there are.

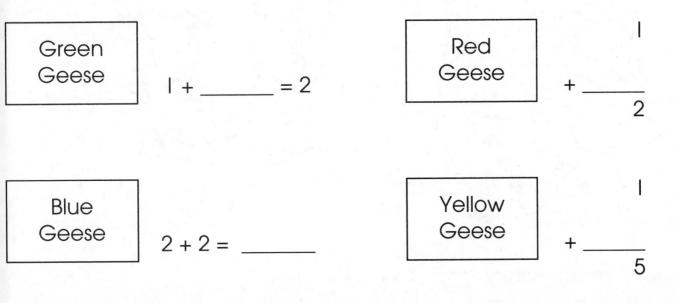

Green Geese	1 + _____ = 2	

Red Geese
1
+ _____
2

Blue Geese	2 + 2 = _____	

Yellow Geese
1
+ _____
5

Addition

Mrs. Murky asked 3 monster girls and 2 monster boys to come to the front of the class. She said, "If I have 3 monster girls and I add 2 monster boys, how many monster children do I have all together?"

Now, do the same problem on the board, but count the 2 boys first.

3   +   2   =   _____

2   +   _____   =   _____

Does it matter which group is counted first? _____

Look at each row of monster children. Write two number problems that describe each row.

_____ + _____ = _____   _____ + _____ = _____

_____ + _____ = _____   _____ + _____ = _____

_____ + _____ = _____   _____ + _____ = _____

Adding and Subtracting

Taking numbers away is called **subtraction**. The symbol used for subtraction is a **minus sign** (–). Look at the pictures below.

6 silly green frogs were sitting on six lily pads.

A big bird flew by and two jumped off into the water.

How many frogs were sitting on the lily pads? _____

How many frogs jumped off? _____

How many frogs were left? _____

Four hungry cats went on a picnic.

Two cats spotted some mice and took off to catch them!

How many cats went on the picnic? _____

How many cats ran after the mice? _____

How many cats were left? _____

Now, write the missing numbers in this subtraction problem.

4 - _____ = _____

You would say:

"Four minus _____ equals _____."

Adding and Subtracting

Benjamin Bunny likes to hop across the numbers. Help him fill in the missing numbers.

Adding 1's:

0 1 2 3 4 5 ___ ___ ___ ___ ___

Adding 2's:

0 2 4 6 8 10 ___ ___ ___ ___ ___

Now, help Benjamin fill in the blanks by subtracting.

Subtracting 1's:

10 9 8 7 6 5 ___ ___ ___ ___ ___

Subtracting 2's:

20 18 16 14 12 10 ___ ___ ___ ___ ___

You and Oliver Opossum have 25¢ to buy some of these toys.

When you buy a toy, cross it out. Then, write it in the table. The first toy is crossed out for you. Each time you buy a toy, subtract it until you have **no more money** to spend.

25¢	–	**4¢**	=	**21¢**
21¢	–	____¢	=	____¢
____¢	–	____¢	=	____¢
____¢	–	____¢	=	____¢
____¢	–	____¢	=	____¢
____¢	–	____¢	=	____¢

Even Numbers

Carla, Mark and Jack have saved their pennies. Help them figure out who has an even number of pennies. An **even number** is a number that can be split into two parts that are the same. Write the number of pennies each child has on the lines. Then, use a red crayon to circle the groups of pennies that have an even number. **Hint:** Try to separate each group into two equal parts.

_____

_____

_____

After lunch, Mrs. Murky wanted to divide her class into 2 groups. Mrs. Murky lined up the boys and girls and told them to count off. The monsters had to shout out their numbers, in order, all the way down the line. Fill in the numbers they shouted.

"Now," said Mrs. Murky, "the **even** numbers will read and the **odd** numbers will do math problems!"

Draw a line from each student to the area where he or she should go to work.

Which group has more? _____

Even and Odd Numbers

The two teams have just arrived at the playing field. Before they start their game, count the monsters on this page and the next to make sure everyone is here.

How many players are wearing **odd** numbers? _____

How many players are wearing **even** numbers? _____

How many coaches are here? _____

Draw a circle around the character who is not a part of the team.

Put the monsters into two teams. All the monsters wearing **odd** numbers are on Team #1. All the monsters wearing **even** numbers are on Team #2. Write their numbers on the team clipboards below.

Team #1

_____

_____

_____

_____

_____

Team #2

_____

_____

_____

_____

_____

Find out which team wins! If the answer is an **odd** number, Team #1 wins. If the answer is an **even** number, Team #2 wins.

$$4 + 2 = \underline{\qquad}$$

Circle all the players who are on the winning team.I

Two-Digit Numbers

Some numbers have **two digits**. The number 15 has **two digits**—the **digit** 1 and the **digit** 5. Look at the pictures below. Hunt for **two-digit** numbers. Draw a circle around each **two-digit** number you find.

Draw a line from each **two-digit** number to its matching word.

16	fourteen
15	nineteen
14	seventeen
19	eighteen
17	fifteen
18	sixteen

Write the missing **two-digit** number in each group. Then, spell that number in the space below. The first one is done for you.

13, **14**, 15   9, 10, _____

fourteen   _____

12, ___, 14   11, _____, 13

_____   _____

Addition

Draw a circle around the groups of 10 bugs in each box. Write the number of tens before the word **tens**. Then, count the bugs that are left. Write the number of ones before the word **ones**. Then, write the sum of the equation. The first one is done for you.

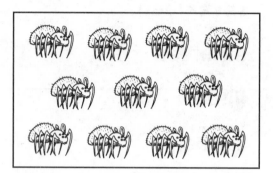 

__1__ ten + __1__ one = __11__   _____ tens + _____ ones = _____

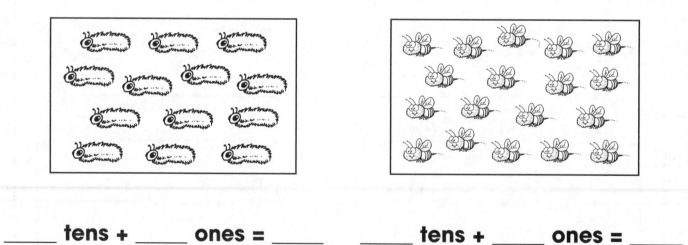

_____ tens + _____ ones = _____   _____ tens + _____ ones = _____

198

Everything for Early Learning Grade 2

Millie and Milo are playing pick-up sticks. Help them count their sticks. Draw a circle around each group of 10 sticks.

How many groups of 10 does Millie have? _____

How many are left over? _____

How many groups of 10 does Milo have? _____

How many are left over? _____

What is Millie's score? _____

What is Milo's score? _____

Who won? _____

Counting to 20

Make the number of shapes in each row below add up to 20 by drawing the correct number of shapes in the empty squares.

Row 1:

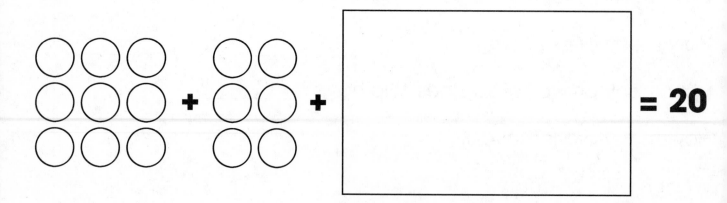

$$\triangle\triangle\triangle\triangle \;+\; \boxed{} \;+\; \triangle\triangle\triangle\triangle\triangle\triangle \;=\; 20$$

Row 2:

$$\bigcirc\bigcirc\bigcirc\bigcirc\bigcirc\bigcirc\bigcirc\bigcirc\bigcirc \;+\; \bigcirc\bigcirc\bigcirc\bigcirc\bigcirc\bigcirc\bigcirc \;+\; \boxed{} \;=\; 20$$

How many equations can you write using the number 20? It can be part of an addition problem or a subtraction problem.

Hint: You may want to use pennies, buttons or lima beans to help you create different equations. Two have been done for you.

$10 + 10 = 20$

$20 - 10 = 10$

Estimation

How many are there of each sea creature in the aquarium? Before you count, guess the number of each creature. This kind of guess is called an **estimate**. Write your **estimates** in the chart below. Then, fill in the rest of the columns in the chart.

	Guess how many. Write your estimate.	Count how many. Write the number.	Did you guess more or less than the real number?

Look at the stars on this page. **Estimate** how many there are.

Write your estimate here: _____

Draw a circle around each group of 10.

How many groups of 10 are there? _____

How many stars are left outside the circle? _____

How many stars are there altogether? _____

Estimation

One hot summer day, Thor decided to take a nap in the shade. He couldn't get to sleep because of all the flies buzzing around his head. He tried to count them, but that made him dizzy! Estimate how many flies are bothering Thor. Write your **estimate** here. _____

Check your **estimate** by counting the flies in groups of 10. Draw a circle around each group of 10.

How many groups of 10 flies are there? _____

How many flies are left over? _____

How many flies are there altogether? _____

Belinda Beastly wants to package buttons in bags of 10, but she is not sure how many bags she will need. She estimates that she will need 5.

What is your estimate? _____

Count the buttons in groups of 10 and draw a "bag" around each group.

How many groups of 10 did you count? _____

How many bags does Belinda need? _____

Pennies

Hector and Hugh, Gerta and Gussie, and Mug and Lug are getting ready to go to the store. They are counting their pennies. Each penny is worth 1 cent.

How much money does Hector have? _____ cents

How much money does Hugh have? _____ cents

How much do Hector and Hugh have? _____ cents

How much do Gerta and Gussie have? _____ cents

How much do Mug and Lug have? _____ cents

Cross out the pair who have the **most** money.

Circle the pair who have the **least** amount of money.

The monsters have counted their money. They are going to buy things at the store. Look at each item on sale. Then, answer each question by drawing an **X** on the pair who have enough money to buy the item.

Who can buy the toothbrush?

_____ Hector and Hugh

_____ Gerta and Gussie

_____ Mug and Lug

Who can buy the grapes?

_____ Hector and Hugh

_____ Gerta and Gussie

_____ Mug and Lug

Who can buy the apple?

_____ Hector and Hugh

_____ Gerta and Gussie

_____ Mug and Lug

Who can buy the doll?

_____ Hector and Hugh

_____ Gerta and Gussie

_____ Mug and Lug

Money

These monsters want to go to the pizza parlor. But they can't go until they know how much they have to spend. Count how much money each monster has. Then, fill in the blanks below.

How much money does Bob have? _____ cents

How much money does Babs have? _____ cents

How much money does Dot have? _____ cents

How much do they have altogether? _____ cents

The monsters are waiting to order. Look at page 208 to find out how much money they have. Then, answer the question below.

MENU

All-You-Can-Eat Pizza	$2.50
Soup	$1.25
Lemonade	$ .25

What can each of the monsters buy with the money

they have? _____

Making Change

Rimsley's mom gave him $1.00 to buy stamps that cost 72¢. What will his change be? _____

Draw pictures to show the coins he could receive as change.

Rimsley might receive these coins in change:

Or he could receive these coins:

Milo needs 1 dollar to buy his favorite lunch at the Slimepit Elementary School cafeteria. He wants a salamander salami sandwich. His mother gave him 10 coins that add up to 1 dollar, and Milo put them in his pocket. His coins include at least 1 quarter, as well as some dimes and nickels. He has no pennies. What coins will Milo use to pay for his lunch? Draw them in the space below.

Money

Dot has learned that she can earn money by recycling. She is saving her money so she can go to the movies. Count the money she earned in January and February by recycling cans, bottles and newspapers. Then, fill in the totals and answer the questions below.

GARBAGE →	🥫	🍾	📰
JANUARY	20¢	50¢	35¢
FEBRUARY	50¢	10¢	22¢
TOTAL			

How much money does she have altogether? _____ cents

Before she went to the movies, she spent:

• 10¢ on candy.
• 20¢ on a balloon.
• 30¢ on a comic book.

How much does she have left? _____ cents

It will cost $1.50 (or 150 cents) to go to the movies. Does she have enough?   YES   NO

Ursula ran into her room after school and flung her bookbag onto her desk. Unfortunately, she knocked over her piggy bank and it broke, spilling all the coins. Can you help her count the coins to see if she has found them all? She knows she had exactly $3.15.

Did Ursula find all of her coins? If not, what is missing? _____

Addition

The monsters are planting a vegetable garden. They're going to do all the work themselves!

How many monsters have a shovel? _____

How many monsters have a hoe? _____

How many tools do you see? _____

- Joot has 2 packets of carrot seeds.
- Moot has 3 packets of pea seeds.
- Hoot has 1 packet of bean seeds.

Find out how many seed packets the monsters have by adding up the numbers below, then fill in the blank.

$$2 + 3 + 1 = \underline{\hspace{2cm}}$$

This chart shows the number of plants each monster is growing. Add up how many of each kind of vegetable they have planted. Fill in the totals at the bottom of the chart. Then, answer the questions below.

Vegetables →			
JOOT	5	1	2
MOOT	1	6	1
HOOT	2	1	4
TOTAL			

How many carrots are the monsters growing? _____

How many peas are the monsters growing? _____

How many beans are the monsters growing? _____

How many plants are growing altogether? _____

Using a Table

Veronica, Ursula and Millie all play on the Slimepit Sluggers softball team. The table below shows how well the girls hit in last week's games.

Use the information in the table to answer these questions.

Which girl had the most hits? _____

How many did she have? _____

What is the total number of hits made by the

girls on Monday? _____   On Wednesday? _____

On Saturday? _____

On which day did the girls perform best as a group? _____

	Veronica	**Ursula**	**Millie**
Monday	4 hits	2 hits	0 hits
Wednesday	3 hits	1 hit	5 hits
Saturday	3 hits	3 hits	3 hits

Geoffrey and Georgia Giraffe love to make graphs.

A **graph** has **rows** of squares. A row goes **across**.

A graph has **columns** of squares, too. A column goes **up** and **down**.

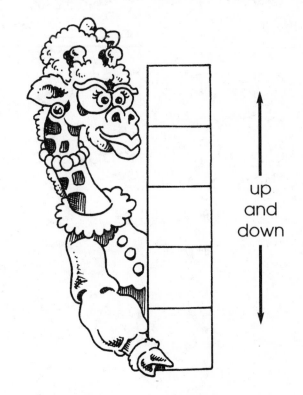

← across →

up and down

Together, the rows and columns make a graph that looks like this:

	Column 1	Column 2	Column 3	Column 4
Row 4				
Row 3				
Row 2				
Row 1				

Make your own graph.

Here is a happy face:

Here is a sad face:

Count up the happy and sad faces you see below.
Then, answer the questions at the bottom of the page.

How many happy faces did you count? _____

How many sad faces did you count? _____

How many faces are there in all? _____

Now, make a graph of the happy and sad faces you counted on page 218. The first row has been done for you. A happy face and a sad face have been drawn in. Fill in the other rows to complete the graph.

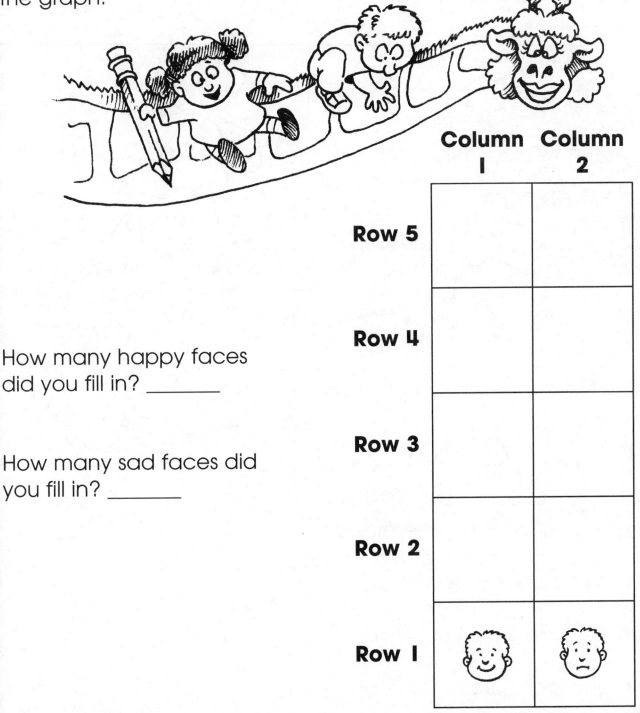

How many happy faces did you fill in? _____

How many sad faces did you fill in? _____

	Column 1	Column 2
Row 5		
Row 4		
Row 3		
Row 2		
Row 1	😊	🙁

Graphing

It's a birthday party! There are lots of good foods to eat.

How many different kinds of food are there? _____
Count up all the foods you see!

How many egg rolls are there above? _____

How many pizzas did you count? _____

How many cakes did you see? _____

How many tacos are there in all? _____

Make a graph of the birthday party foods. Use the number of each food you counted to fill in your graph. Draw the pictures in the correct columns. The first row has been done for you.

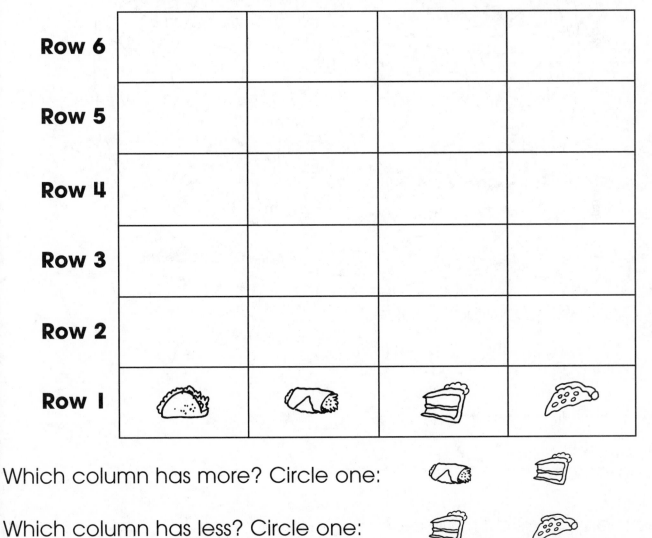

	Column 1	Column 2	Column 3	Column 4
Row 6				
Row 5				
Row 4				
Row 3				
Row 2				
Row 1	🌮	🌯	🍰	🍕

Which column has more? Circle one:

Which column has less? Circle one:

The cookies below are in the shape of four different animals. Before you count them, estimate how many animals there are

in all: _____

Now, count the animal cookies!

How many giraffes did you count? _____

How many lions are there in all? _____

How many turtles are there? _____

How many dogs do you see? _____

Complete the graph below. Use the number of each animal you counted to fill in the rows with the missing pictures of turtles and dogs. The giraffes and lions have been filled in for you.

	Column 1	Column 2	Column 3	Column 4	Column 5
giraffe	🦒	🦒	🦒		
lion	🦁	🦁			
turtle					
dog					

Which animal cookie is there the most of? _____

Which animal cookie is there the fewest of? _____

Two kinds of cookies have the same number.

How many are there? _____

Graphing

Ursula grew a great deal the past year! Help her make a graph that shows how much she grew each month. On page 225, color in one box for each inch she grew.

- January, 3 inches
- February, 0 inches
- March, 1 inch
- April, 2 inches
- May, 2 inches
- June, 0 inches
- July, 1 inch
- August, 0 inches
- September, 4 inches
- October, 1 inch
- November, 1 inch
- December, 2 inches

Inches Grown

January				
February				
March				
April				
May				
June				
July				
August				
September				
October				
November				
December				

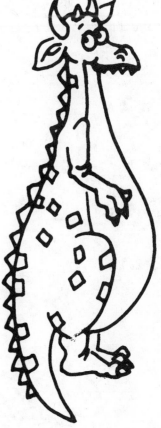

How many inches did Ursula grow altogether? _____

Did Ursula grow more in the first half of the year or in the last half of

the year? _____

Addition

The monsters love to bake sweet things. Their favorites are snail tarts, slime cookies and thorny cream puffs. Simon and Stella are planning what they are each going to bake.

Fill in the blanks below to find out how many sweet things Simon will bake.

3 + 2 = _____

6 + 3 = _____

4 + 3 = _____

TOTAL _____

Fill in the blanks below to find out how many sweet things Stella will bake.

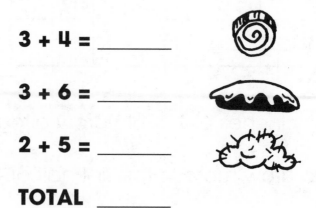

3 + 4 = _____

3 + 6 = _____

2 + 5 = _____

TOTAL _____

While Simon and Stella were in the back washing dishes. Simon's twin nephews came to visit. The nephews gobbled down some treats. They knocked over some bowls. They even sat on some pastries!

Simon made a list of all the sweets he and Stella lost. Can you help him add up the ruined sweets, then put the totals in the boxes below?

Sweets →					
STELLA	6	4	9	5	7
SIMON	6	3	1	2	2
TOTAL					

Addition/Subtraction

Once upon a time, 2 very hungry monsters named Zort and Zerta went looking for tasty things to put in their soup. Zort found 5 snails asleep under a bush.

"Mmm, delicious!" he said. He put the snails into his pockets. Zerta found 3 rotten apples in the dirt by a fence.

"Terrific!" she snorted, stuffing the apples into her basket.

They headed home to their kitchen, but on the way, 1 tricky snail slowly crawled out of Zort's pocket and escaped.

How many things can the monsters put in their soup? Complete the number sentences below.

_____ 🐌 + _____ 🍎 = _____ 🐌 − _____ 🐌 = _____ 🐌

What a feast! Eight monsters are eating a delicious dinner at the Monster Cafe. The chef has cooked his favorite meal of snails, worms and dirt sandwiches!

Everything was going fine, until . . .

Twister left to answer the telephone.
Toot went home because she forgot her money.
Buster left to pick up his sister at the bus stop.

How many monsters had to leave the table? _____

After Twister, Toot and Buster left, how many chairs were

empty? _____

How many monsters were left at the table? _____

Subtraction

Moot, the cook at the Monster Cafe, is working very hard. He has many orders to fill. Look on the menu to see what the most popular dishes are.

Count all the orders below. How many orders does Moot have

to fill? _____

Moot worked very fast and filled:

1 soup order, 2 pasta orders and 3 sandwich orders

How many orders does Moot have left to fill?

_____ more soup order(s)

_____ more pasta order(s)

_____ more sandwich order(s)

The monster parade is about to begin. But only 6 monsters are ready to march! Read what happened to the missing marchers. Then, answer the questions at the bottom of the page.

- I monster broke her toe.

- 2 monsters lost their music.

- I monster caught a cold.

- 2 monsters were too big to fit into their uniforms.

How many monsters went home? _____

How many monsters would be in the parade if all the marchers

came? _____

Monsters love parades! There are so many monsters, nobody can see what they look like—except for Fred. Fred took his binoculars up in a tree to see how many monsters were at the parade.

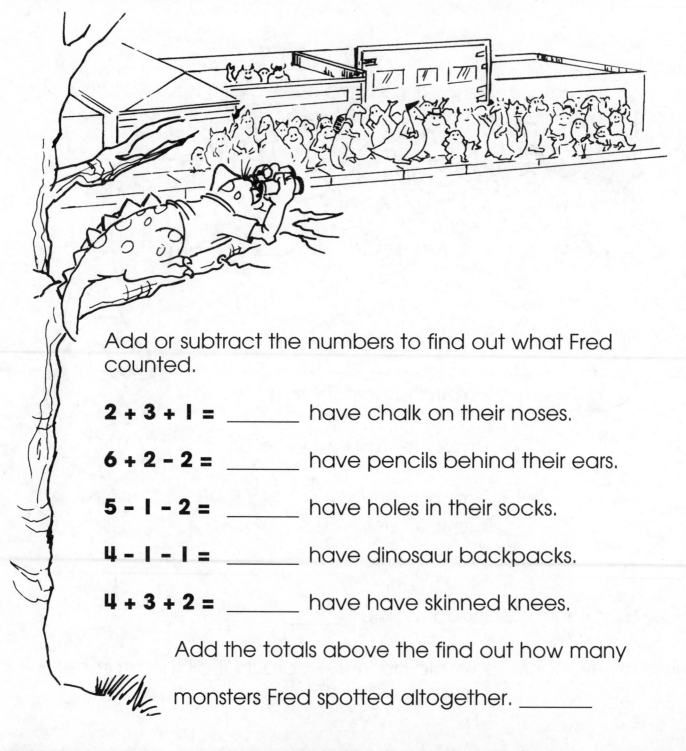

Add or subtract the numbers to find out what Fred counted.

2 + 3 + 1 = _____ have chalk on their noses.

6 + 2 – 2 = _____ have pencils behind their ears.

5 – 1 – 2 = _____ have holes in their socks.

4 – 1 – 1 = _____ have dinosaur backpacks.

4 + 3 + 2 = _____ have have skinned knees.

Add the totals above the find out how many

monsters Fred spotted altogether. _____

Try to figure out the following problem as you read it. Do the adding and subtracting in your head. Use a pencil and paper only if you get stuck!

Mary and Marvin asked all their friends to come to the park to play baseball. Mary, Marvin and 10 other monsters arrived at the park at 10 o'clock. 3 more monsters arrived at 11:00. At 12:00, 4 monsters had to go home for lunch, and I had to leave for a dentist appointment. At 1:00, the McGuire twins arrived, along with Marvin's cousin Milton.

How many monsters were at the park at 11:00? _____

How many monsters were at the park at 12:00? _____

How many monsters were at the park at 1:00? _____

Subtraction

Mibby the monster wins every card game she plays! It's the start of a new game. Look at all the cards in her hand.

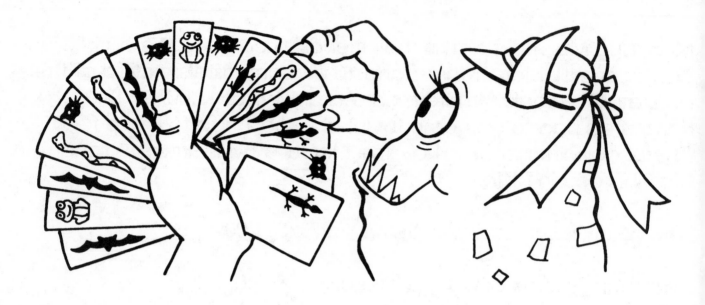

How many cards
does she have? _____

Before the game is over,
she has to give:

- 3 black cat cards to May.
- 2 snake cards to Jud.
- 3 bat cards to Wooster.
- 1 frog card to Mitsy.

How many cards
does Mibby have left? _____

Rodney is sad because it is raining and he can't go out to play. He is sitting by the window, counting the raindrops as they land on the glass.

16 raindrops are on the window as Rodney begins to count. 4 of the raindrops slide away and soon disappear. 5 new drops hit the window. How many raindrops are on the window now? _____

8 of the raindrops slide away, but 2 new raindrops hit the window. Now, how many raindrops can Rodney see on the glass? _____

9 of these raindrops slide away. How many are left? _____

2 raindrops race each other to the bottom of the window pane. Now, how many raindrops does Rodney see? _____

Addition

Play this baseball game to test yourself on time and addition!

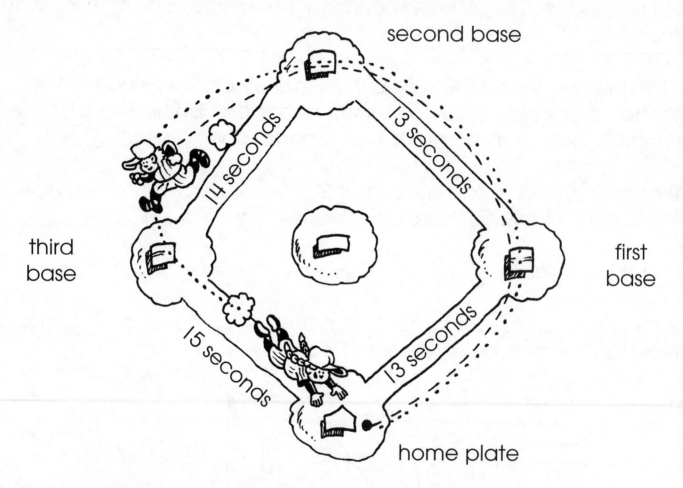

1. Samuel hits the ball and makes it all the way to third base! How long does it take him to get there? (**Note:** seconds = sec.)

_____ sec. + _____ sec. + _____ sec. = _____ sec.
(to first base)   (to second base)   (to third base)

2. Jenny hits a home run! How long does it take her to touch all the bases and reach home plate?

____ sec. + ____ sec. + ____ sec. = ____ sec. = ____ sec.
(to first base) (to second base) (to third base) (to home plate)

Some of the monster children went to the zoo on Sunday. They took pictures of their favorite animals.

- Millie took pictures of 4 elephants, 16 penguins and 11 wallabies.
- Milo took pictures of 18 wallabies, 9 monkeys and 3 tigers.
- Jed took pictures of 21 penguins, 7 giraffes and 4 monkeys.

Which monster took the most pictures? _____

Which monster took the fewest pictures? _____

How many different kinds of animals were

photographed? _____

Subtraction

Once there was a monster named Miles, who spent every day playing marbles. He kept his 20 favorite marbles in a beautiful marble bag. One day, he grabbed his marbles and went to play with his friends.

At Wilbur's house, he lost 10 marbles. How many marbles did he have left?

Fill in the blank and carry down the total to the next blank.

20 - 10 = _____

At Rosie's house, he lost 2 more! Carry down the total to the next blank.

_____ **- 2 =** _____

At Fuddy's house, he lost 3 more!

_____ **- 3 =** _____

At Matilda's house, he lost 4 more!

_____ **- 4 =** _____

What a sad day for Miles!

How many marbles did he have left? _____

Wilbur put the marbles he won from Miles into a bag. 5 of the marbles are white and 5 of them are black. Wilbur wants to give his brother Warren 2 of the marbles, but Warren wants the marbles to be the same color. If Wilbur reaches into his bag without looking, how many marbles will he have to pull out to make sure that he gets 2 of the same color?

The first marble Wilbur pulls out of the bag is black. Next, he pulls out a white marble. The third marble is sure to match one of the first 2.

Why?

_____

Is it possible that Wilbur could pull out matching marbles in 2 tries? Why or why not? _____

_____

Probability

Jag has a penny. He is playing heads or tails. He would like you to play, too.

Find a penny around your house and flip it into the air. Let it land on a table. Look to see if it landed "heads up" or "tails up." Make a mark in the correct column on the tally chart. Do this 10 times. Does your tally chart look the same as Jag's? Keep flipping the penny and making marks.

How do you think your chart will look if you flip the penny 50 times? Why? Try it to see if your prediction is correct.

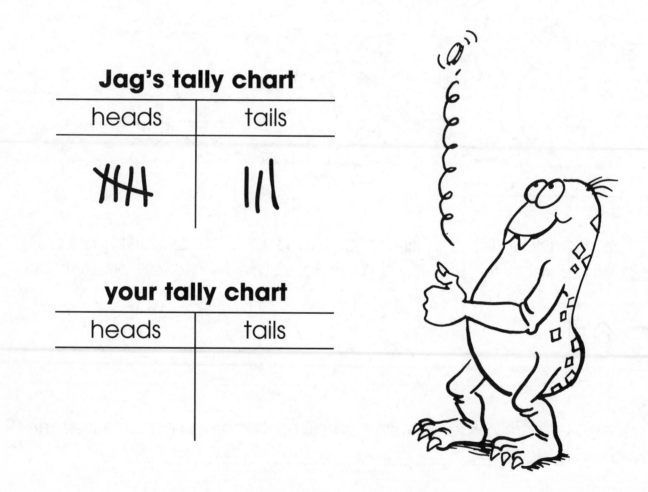

Jag's tally chart

heads	tails
✖︎✖︎✖︎	|||

your tally chart

heads	tails

Mit has 4 kinds of shoes and 3 kinds of socks. She has made this chart to help her see what the socks and shoes will look like together.

How many different sock-and-shoe combinations can

she make? _____

(**Hint:** It will help to draw each sock-and-shoe combination in the squares provided.)

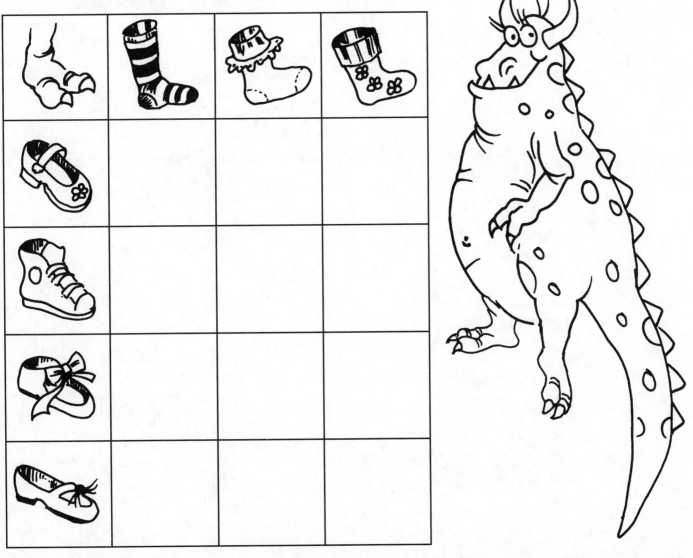

Time

The **little hand** on a clock points to the **hour**. The **big hand** points to the **minutes**. When the big hand reaches 12, a new hour begins. Look at all the things Juan is doing today. Write the number that tells the time of each activity. The first one is done for you.

It is ___6___ o'clock.

It is _____ o'clock.

It is _____ o'clock.

It is _____ o'clock.

It is _____ o'clock.

It is _____ o'clock.

Everything for Early Learning Grade 2

When the big hand is on the 6, it is on the **half hour**. A half hour is 30 minutes, or halfway between one hour and the next. You write it as **:30**. For example, 7:30 is halfway between 7 o'clock and 8 o'clock.

Alice is always half an hour late. Complete each clock to show what time she does each activity described below. Then, write the time on the lines below the clocks. The first one is done for you.

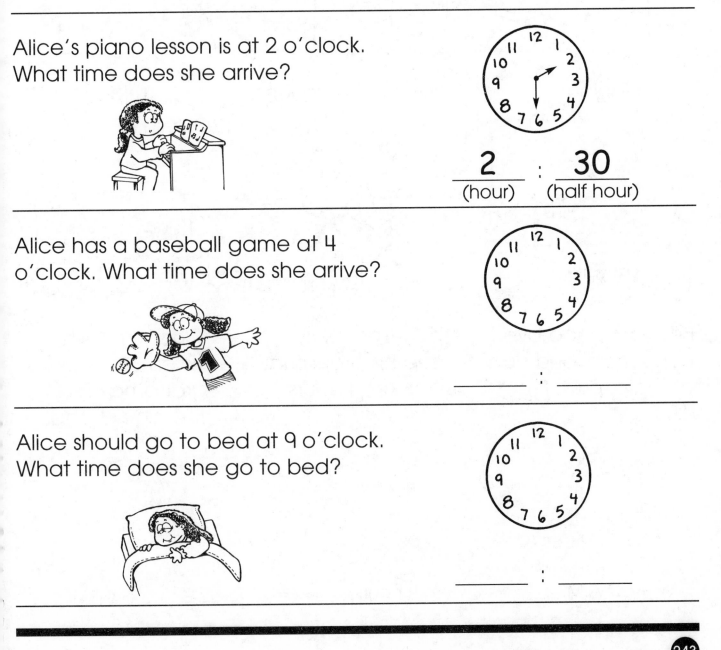

Alice's piano lesson is at 2 o'clock. What time does she arrive?

__2__ : __30__
(hour)   (half hour)

Alice has a baseball game at 4 o'clock. What time does she arrive?

_____ : _____

Alice should go to bed at 9 o'clock. What time does she go to bed?

_____ : _____

When something happens between 12:00 midnight and 12:00 noon, we say it is **A.M.**

When something happens between 12:00 noon and 12:00 midnight, it is **P.M.**

midnight   noon   noon   midnight

12:00 A.M.   12:00 P.M.

Billy says good-bye to his mom and dad at the airport. It is 9:00 A.M.

Billy flies away to see his grandma. It takes 4 hours.

What time is it when Billy sees his grandma? Fill in the clock hands.

   +   4 hours   =   

9:00 A.M.   +   4 hours   =   _____ ___.___.

Bobbie is going to visit his grandma, too. Show what time he completes each part of his trip by adding the correct number of hours to the times below. Write your answer on the lines. Then, draw that time on the clock. Include A.M. or P.M. in your answer. The first one is done for you.

Bobbie leaves his house at 7 o'clock in the morning. It takes 2 hours for his dad to drive him to the airport. What time does he arrive at the airport?

7:00 A.M. + ___2___ hours = **9:00 A.M.**

Bobbie's plane leaves the airport at 10 o'clock in the morning. It arrives 4 hours later. What time does his plane land?

10:00 A.M. + _____ hours = _____

Then, Bobbie takes a bus at 3:00 in the afternoon. He arrives at his grandma's house 1 hour later. What time does he arrive?

3:00 P.M. + _____ hour = _____

Millie and Maggie have decided to meet for dinner at the Disgusting Diner at 6:00.

If it takes Millie 20 minutes to paint her toenails and 2 minutes to walk to the diner, what time should she start getting ready?

_____

If it takes Maggie 15 minutes to brush her fangs and 3 minutes to walk to the diner, what time should she start getting ready?

_____

Maggie wants to go to Millie's house for a visit after dinner. How long will it take her to walk back to her home from Millie's house?

_____

If she leaves at 8:20, what time will she arrive home?

_____

Ursula began to make 3 bracelets at 6 o'clock. It takes 15 minutes to make each bracelet. If Ursula does not take a break, at what time will she finish the 3 bracelets? Fill in the clock face below to show that time.

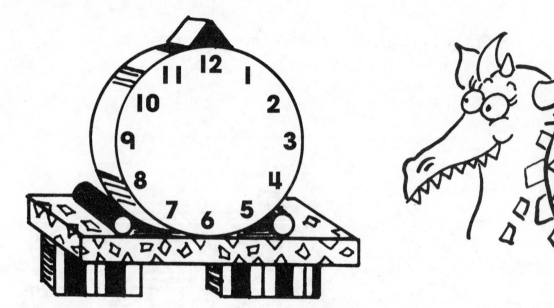

If Ursula takes a 5-minute break after completing each bracelet, at what time will she be finished with all 3? Fill in the clock face below to show that time.

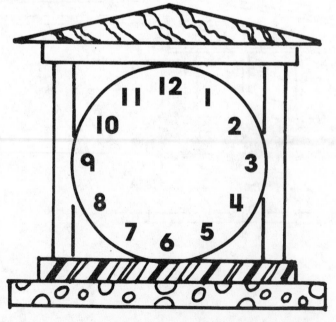

Becky had a busy day. Look at her activities. What did she do first? What did she do second? What did she do third? Draw a line form the correct word to the picture.

first

second

third

Maggie, Fred and Gus went to a birthday party. They each brought flowers and a gift. Use the clues to find out the order in which they arrived at the party and what each one brought. Fill in the chart on page 251.

- Maggie did not arrive last.

- The monster who brought mugwort arrived first.

- The monster who brought dandelions arrived before the monster who brought some stinky cheese.

- Gus arrived after Fred.

Arrived	First	Second	Third
Maggie			
Fred			
Gus			
Gifts	Dandelions	Mugwort	Stinky Cheese
Maggie			
Fred			
Gus			

Ordinal Numbers

Nancy is learning her **ordinal numbers**. Help her by drawing the correct shapes in the boxes below. Follow the instructions above each box.

1 2 3 4 5

Draw the third shape.

Draw the first shape.

Draw the fifth shape.

Draw the fourth shape.

Robbie the robot and his pal Roger are made of many different-shaped objects. Look at all the shapes on their bodies. Then, follow the directions below.

Use a green crayon to color all the circles on their bodies. This is a circle: ◯ .

Use an orange crayon to color all the ovals on their bodies. This is an oval: ⬭ .

Color the other shapes any way you like.

Shapes

Some shapes have sides. How many sides does each shape below have? Write the number of sides inside each shape.

square

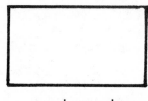
rectangle

triangle

Help Robbie get to his space car by tracing the path that has only squares, rectangles and triangles.

Hint: You may want to draw an **X** on all the other shapes. This will help you see the path more clearly.

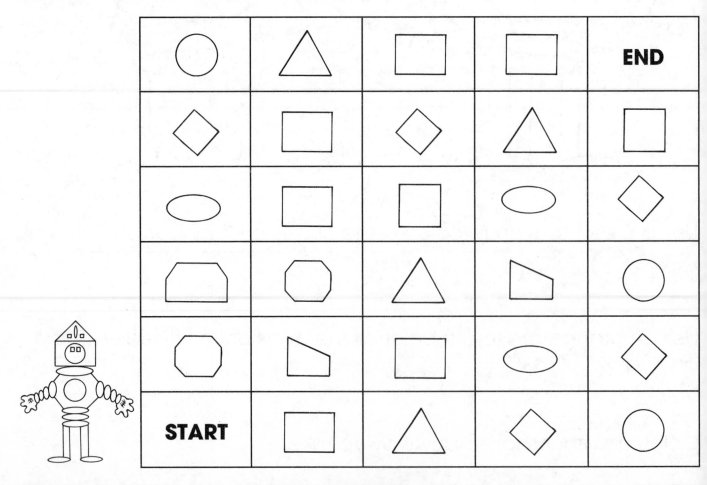

Look at the grid below. All the shapes have straight sides, like a square.

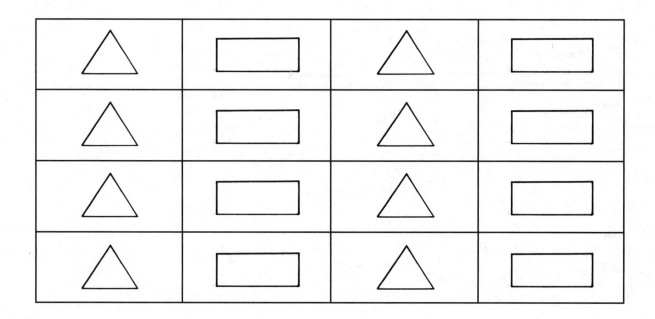

Now, make your own pattern grid. Use only shapes with straight sides like the grid above. The grid has been started for you.

Shapes

Geometrus is a monster made of many different shapes. Look carefully to discover how many of each shape Geometrus has.

☐ There are _____ squares.

△ There are _____ triangles.

▭ There are _____ rectangles.

⬠ There are _____ pentagons.

⬡ There are _____ octagons.

○ There are _____ circles.

⬭ There are _____ ovals.

Mrs. Murky has asked each of the children to design a doghouse for a Monster Mutt. Can you help them? The house must contain at least 3 of the shapes you found on page 256. Draw your design in the space below.

Counting to 100

Mrs. Murky has asked the monster boys and girls to fill in the number chart on page 259 from 1 to 100. Then, use these clues to help the monsters find a secret number!

- The number is even.

- It is greater than 17.

- It is less than 80.

- When the number is separated into groups of 10, there are 2 left over.

- The numeral in the tens place is 1 greater than the numeral in the ones place.

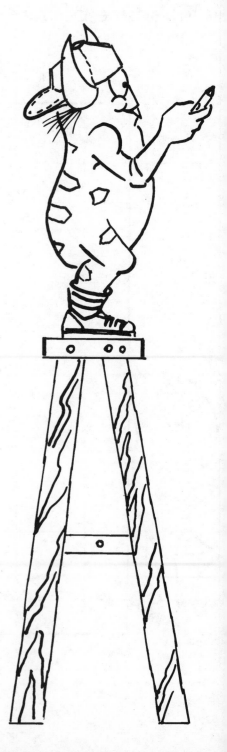

1		3		5		7		9	
	12		14		16		18		20
21		23		25		27		29	
	32		34		36		38		40
41		43		45		47		49	
	52		54		56		58		60
61		63		65		67		69	
	72		74		76		78		80
81		83		85		87		89	
	92		94		96		98		100

Multiplication

The monster babies are having fun at their play group. They like to play with blocks the best. Look at all the tall towers they have built!

Use multiplication to find out how many blocks are in each monster's tall towers.

_____	**x**	_____	**=**	_____
number of towers		blocks in each tower		total number of blocks

_____	**x**	_____	**=**	_____
number of towers		blocks in each tower		total number of blocks

_____	**x**	_____	**=**	_____
number of towers		blocks in each tower		total number of blocks

Look at the monsters on this page. Use multiplication to find out how many fingers each monster has.

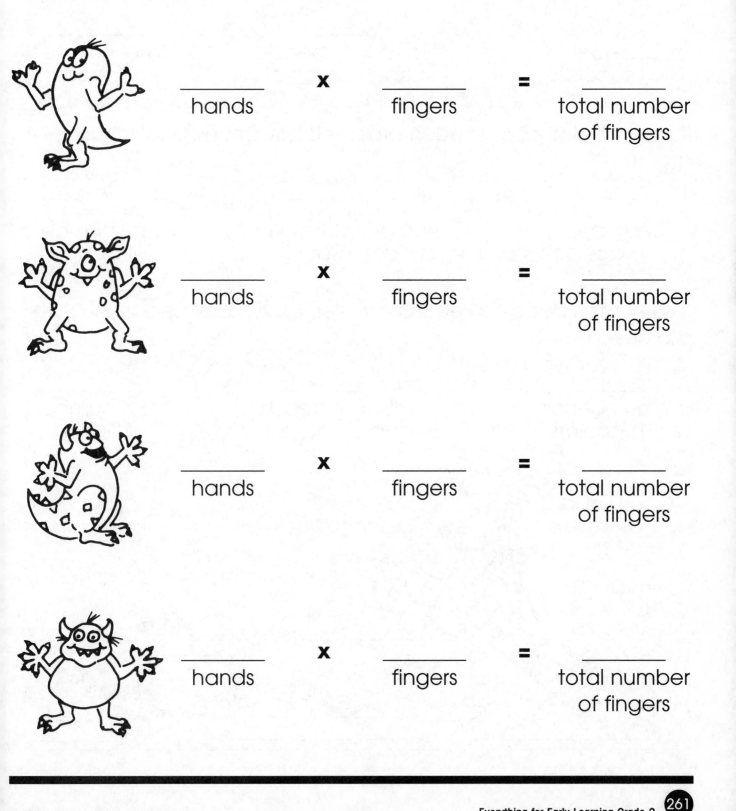

_____ x _____ = _____
hands   fingers   total number
                          of fingers

_____ x _____ = _____
hands   fingers   total number
                          of fingers

_____ x _____ = _____
hands   fingers   total number
                          of fingers

_____ x _____ = _____
hands   fingers   total number
                          of fingers

Multiplication

Ursula is busy making 3 bracelets for her friends. If she puts 3 beads on each bracelet, how many beads will she need?

_____ **x** _____ **=** _____

number of
bracelets

number of beads
in each bracelet

total number
of beads

If she puts 4 beads on each bracelet, how many beads will she need?

_____ **x** _____ **=** _____

number of
bracelets

number of beads
in each bracelet

total number
of beads

If she puts 5 beads on each bracelet, how many beads will she need?

_____ **x** _____ **=** _____

number of
bracelets

number of beads
in each bracelet

total number
of beads

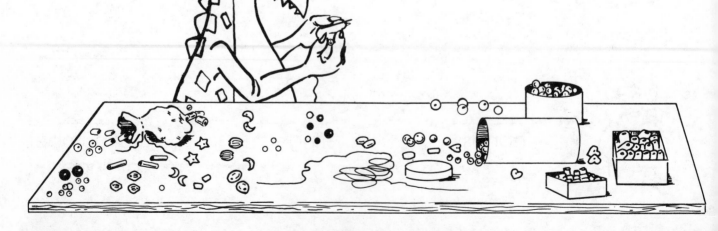

If she puts 6 beads on each bracelet, how many beads will she need?

_____ **x** _____ **=** _____

number of
bracelets

number of beads
in each bracelet

total number
of beads

If she puts 7 beads on each bracelet, how many beads will she need?

_____ **x** _____ **=** _____

number of
bracelets

number of beads
in each bracelet

total number
of beads

If she puts 8 beads on each bracelet, how many beads will she need?

_____ **x** _____ **=** _____

number of
bracelets

number of beads
in each bracelet

total number
of beads

If she puts 9 beads on each bracelet, how many beads will she need?

_____ **x** _____ **=** _____

number of
bracelets

number of beads
in each bracelet

total number
of beads

Multiplication

Ursula's friends loved the bracelets she made. They want her to make them some necklaces to match. She has gone to the store to buy more beads. Help her choose the beads for the necklaces.

Ursula wants to put 4 beads on each necklace. How much will each necklace cost if she chooses:

- the 4¢ beads? _____   • the 7¢ beads? _____

- the 5¢ beads? _____   • the 8¢ beads? _____

- the 6¢ beads? _____   • the 9¢ beads? _____

Jag is counting his nickels. Help him find out how much money he has in each stack of nickels. Do the multiplication by following the examples below. Remember that each nickel is worth 5 cents!

1	x	5	=	5		_____	x	_____	=	_____
2	x	5	=	_____		_____	x	_____	=	_____
_____	x	_____	=	_____		_____	x	_____	=	_____
_____	x	_____	=	_____		_____	x	_____	=	_____
						_____	x	_____	=	_____

Multiplication

The trolls came during the night. They left a secret number combination in the square rocks. Solve the math problems below to help the monsters unlock the door to Troll Mountain. (**Hint:** It will help you to count the boxes in each problem.)

4 x 2 = _____

4 x 3 = _____

3 x _____ = _____

4 x _____ = _____

Add up the 4 final answers to the problems the trolls left on the previous page to open the mountain door. If the total of the 4 answers is correct (the answer is upside down, below), the door will unlock. Write the answer on the combination lock below.

(The secret number combination is 42.)

Multiplication/Addition

Datto decided it was time to clean his closet. But, after he got to work, Datto found little monster bugs everywhere! Fill in the blanks below to help him find out how many bugs are in his closet.

Datto has 4 ties and on every tie there are 2 bugs. _____ bugs are on his ties.

Datto has 3 sweaters and on every sweater there is 1 bug.

_____ bugs are on his sweaters.

Datto has 2 hats and on every hat there are 5 bugs. _____ bugs are on his hats.

Datto has 6 shirts and on every shirt there are 2 bugs. _____ bugs are on his shirts.

How many monsters bugs did Datto find altogether in his

closet? _____

Rimsley is helping out at his mom's office. She has asked him to mail some letters.

Rimsley needs to buy 2 stamps for each envelope. If there are 9 envelopes, how many stamps will he need? _____

Each stamp costs 4 cents. How much will Rimsley have to spend on stamps to mail all the letters? _____

Multiplication

One Saturday, Cosmos went shopping in the city with his mother. He tried to count the windows in the tall buildings, but it made him dizzy. Explain to Cosmos how he could use multiplication to figure out how many windows there are on each building.

_____

_____

_____

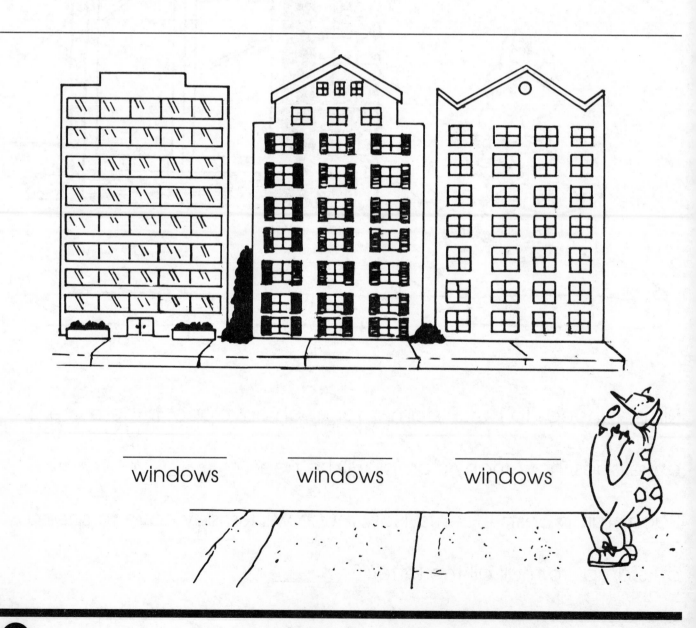

_____   _____   _____

windows   windows   windows

Everything for Early Learning Grade 2

Read each problem. Then, write a number sentence and draw apples in the basket to show your answer.

If the farmer picks 1 apple off each tree, how many apples will he have?

_____ X _____ = _____

If the farmer picks 3 apples off each tree, how many apples will he have?

_____ X _____ = _____

If the farmer picks 4 apples off each tree, how many apples will he have?

_____ X _____ = _____

Multiplication

The monsters are having a wonderful time at the farm! Everybody has a special job to do. Solve the problems below to find out how many monsters are needed for each job.

There are 4 cows to be milked. Each cow needs 3 monsters to milk it. How many monsters get to milk the cows?

_____ monsters are needed to milk the cows.

There are 7 horses on the farm. Each horse can carry 2 monsters at the same time. How many monsters can ride the horses at one time?

_____ monsters can ride at the same time.

This monster farmer is going to pick some apples off his trees. He has 3 trees. If he picks 2 apples off each tree, how many apples will he have in his basket?

Draw the apples in the basket. Below it, write a number sentence that explains your answer.

_____	x	_____	=	_____
apples from each tree		trees		total apples

10 monsters want to play on the monkey bars, but only 3 monsters are allowed on a bar at the same time.

Are there enough bars for all the monsters to play? _____

Explain your answer.

_____

_____

These 6 monsters are hungry! Their picnic lunch is ready! Look at the picture and count each of the food items. Then, divide the food equally to find out what each monster will eat. Write the answers on the lines.

_____ lollipops   _____ cupcakes   _____ apples

_____ carrots   _____ drinks

Mrs. Murky wants to give flowers to the 6 best spellers in her class. She wants to put at least 5 flowers in each bouquet.

Does she have enough flowers in her garden? _____

Could she put more flowers in each bouquet? Explain your answer.

_____

_____

The monsters are saving their money to go to the amusement park next week.

Look at the chart to see how much money they earn each day for each chore. Then, answer the questions below to find out how much money the monsters will have for the amusement park.

They swept floors on 3 different days. How much did they earn? _____ cents

The monsters dusted on 4 different days. How much did they earn? _____ cents

They mopped the floors on the same days they swept the floors. How much did they earn for mopping? _____ cents

They washed dishes on 6 different days. How much did they earn? _____ cents

How much money did the monsters earn for the whole week? _____ cents

Chores	Money
	10¢
	20¢
	40¢
	50¢

Multiplication

The monsters, with their money in their pockets, ran all the way to the amusement park. They want to buy tickets to go on the rides.

Ferris wheel   20¢
Merry-go-round   10¢
Pony ride   50¢
Bumper car   15¢

Look on page 277 to find out how much they earned: _____ cents

How much money would they spend on each ride if all 3 monsters go on every ride once?

Fill in the blanks below.

 Ferris wheel tickets   _____ cents

Merry-go-round tickets   _____ cents

Pony ride tickets   _____ cents

Bumper car tickets   _____ cents

On Saturday, the Slimepit Elementary School basketball team played against the team from Grubwater Street School. Use the information found in this chart to answer the questions below.

	Slimepit attempted	Made	Grubwater attempted	Made
1-point shots (free throws)	12	8	10	6
2-point shots	28	17	33	18
3-point shots	7	4	4	3

Which team won the game? _____

By how many points? _____

If both teams had made every free throw, which team would

have won? _____

By how many points? _____

Fractions

The monsters are getting in shape Look below and on page 281 to see the different ways they are working out. Then, answer the questions on page 281.

Answer the questions and fill in the blanks below. The first one is done for you.

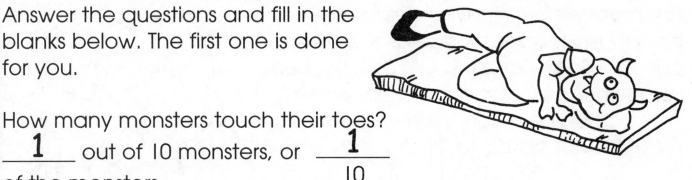

How many monsters touch their toes?
___1___ out of 10 monsters, or ___1___
of the monsters.   10

How many monsters hang upside down?
_____ out of 10 monsters, or _____
of the monsters.   10

How many monsters run on the treadmill?
_____ out of 10 monsters, or _____
of the monsters.   10

How many monsters lift weights?
_____ out of 10 monsters, or _____
of the monsters.   10

How many monsters do leg lifts?
_____ out of 10 monsters, or _____
of the monsters.   10

Fractions

The monsters are studying the Moon. It changes its appearance as the month goes by. Sometimes the full moon is seen. Sometimes only part of it is seen. When only part of the Moon is showing, it is a **fraction** of its full size.

Help the monsters learn fractions by filling in the blanks below.

Pretend the Moon is divided into 2 equal parts.

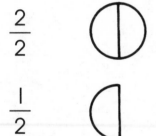

$\frac{2}{2}$ The Moon is full. The monsters see both of its 2 parts.

$\frac{1}{2}$ This is a half moon. The monsters see only _____ of its 2 parts.

What if you divided the Moon into 4 equal parts?

$\frac{4}{4}$ The Moon is full. The monsters can see all 4 of its _____ parts.

$\frac{3}{4}$ The Moon is almost full. The monsters can see _____ of the 4 parts.

$\frac{}{4}$ The Moon is half full. The monsters can see _____ of the 4 parts.

$\frac{}{4}$ The Moon is almost gone. Only _____ part is left.

The monsters are on their way to the farthest part of the galaxy. Answer the questions below.

How many objects do they see out the window? _____

How many rockets do they see? _____

How many comets do they see? _____

How many planets to they see? _____

How many stars do they see? _____

Look at the picture above. Then, fill in the blanks below.

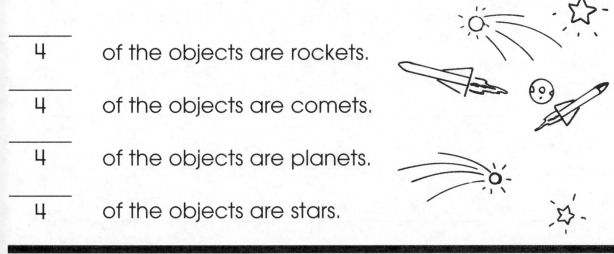

_____ of the objects are rockets.
   4

_____ of the objects are comets.
   4

_____ of the objects are planets.
   4

_____ of the objects are stars.
   4

Fractions

One day, the monsters went to the pizza stand for a snack.

- Mug ate $\frac{1}{2}$ of a pizza.

- Lug ate $\frac{2}{4}$ of a pizza.

- Gug ate $\frac{3}{6}$ of a pizza.

Color the portion of pizza that each monster ate.

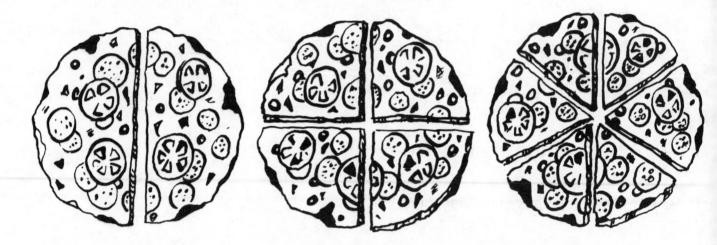

Which monster ate the most pizza?

Explain your answer.

_____

_____

_____

_____

One morning, Mrs. Murky asks her class:

"Which would you rather have, $\frac{1}{2}$ of a candy bar

or $\frac{2}{4}$ of a candy bar?"

Which would you rather have? Explain your answer.

_____

_____

_____

Fractions

Help the monsters use the candy bars below to answer the questions on page 287.

Which is more, $\frac{2}{3}$ or $\frac{3}{4}$? _____

Which is more, $\frac{2}{4}$ or $\frac{3}{6}$? _____

Which is more, $\frac{1}{2}$ or $\frac{3}{5}$? _____

Which is more, $\frac{2}{6}$ or $\frac{1}{3}$? _____

Which is more, $\frac{3}{4}$ or $\frac{4}{5}$? _____

Which is more, $\frac{4}{6}$ or $\frac{2}{3}$? _____

Fractions

Suji and Samantha had Millie and Milo over to play after school. Their mother gave them a plate of cookies to share. If they divide the cookies equally, how many cookies will there be for each monster? Draw the cookies on the plates to show how many each monster gets.

Rodney, Jed and Ursula had a pizza party. They ordered 1 large fish-eye pizza and 1 large toadstool pizza. Draw lines through the pizzas to divide them equally into slices. Color the pizza slices in 3 colors, 1 for each monster, to show how many slices each monster gets.

How many slices will each monster get? _____

Measurement

Mrs. Murky shows the students a map of the Slimepit Elementary School play yard. Each box shows 1 square meter. Two half-boxes show 1 square meter.

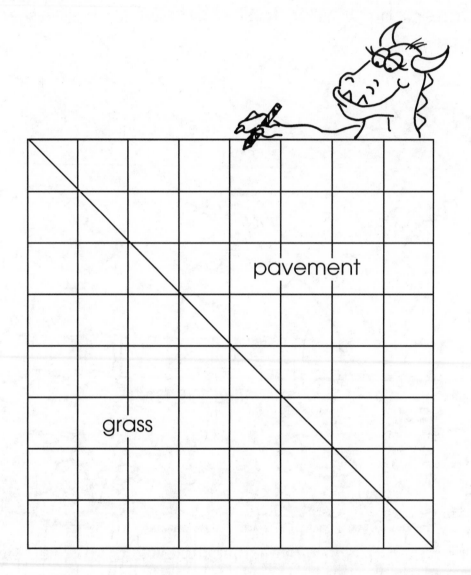

She asks them these questions:

How many square meters of the play yard are pavement? _____

How many square meters of the play yard are grass? _____

MATH GAMES
AND
PUZZLES

Addition

John and Emily are playing tic-tac-toe. John is **O** and Emily is **X**. Follow the instructions below to find out who wins the game. The winner is the player who gets 3 **X**'s or 3 **O**'s in any row—down (↓), across (→) or diagonally (↗ ↘).

- John puts an **O** on the sum of 5 + 2.
- Emily puts an **X** on the sum of 3 + 2.
- John puts an **O** on the sum of 1 + 0.
- Emily puts an **X** on the sum of 2 + 2.
- John puts an **O** on the sum of 2 + 1.
- Emily puts an **X** on the sum of 1 + 1.
- John puts an **O** on the sum of 2 + 4.
- Emily puts an **X** on the sum of 4 + 4.
- John puts an **O** on the sum of 7 + 2.

3	8	7
2	9	5
1	6	4

Who won the game? _____

Spike the dog and Mookie the cat are playing tic-tac-toe. Spike is **O**. Mookie is **X**. Find out who wins the game by following the directions below.

- Spike puts an **O** on the sum of 10 + 2.
- Mookie puts an **X** on the sum of 13 + 4.
- Spike puts an **O** on the sum of 10 + 10.
- Mookie puts an **X** on the sum of 5 + 8.
- Spike puts an **O** on the sum of 9 + 6.
- Mookie puts an **X** on the sum of 13 + 5.
- Spike puts an **O** on the sum of 9 + 10.
- Mookie puts an **X** on the sum of 8 + 2.
- Spike puts an **O** on the sum of 3 + 11.

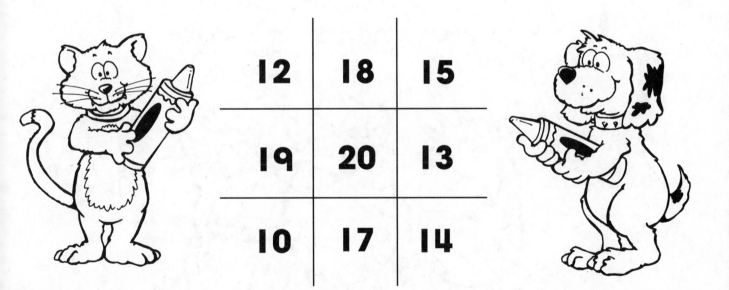

12	18	15
19	20	13
10	17	14

Who won the game? _____

Multiplication

Bugsy and Bonnie are playing tic-tac-toe. Bugsy is **X** and Bonnie is **O**. Solve these problems to see who wins! Remember that a product is the answer to a multiplication problem.

- Put an **X** on the product of 3 x 2.

- Put an **O** on the product of 4 x 3.

- Put an **X** on the product of 5 x 1.

- Put an **O** on the product of 2 x 4.

- Put an **X** on the product of 5 x 3.

- Put an **O** on the product of 5 x 4.

- Put an **X** on the product of 3 x 3.

- Put an **O** on the product of 4 x 4.

Who won the game? _____

Multiplication

Veronica and Jed are playing tic-tac-toe. Veronica is **X** and Jed is **O**. Solve these problems to see who wins! Remember that a product is the answer to a multiplication problem.

- Put an **X** on the product of 6 x 3.

- Put an **O** on the product of 6 x 4.

- Put an **X** on the product of 6 x 5.

- Put an **O** on the product of 6 x 6.

- Put an **X** on the product of 6 x 7.

- Put an **O** on the product of 6 x 8.

- Put an **X** on the product of 6 x 9.

- Put an **O** on the product of 6 x 2.

30	12	24
54	18	42
48	6	36

Who won the game? _____

Multiplication

Rimsley and Maggie are playing SLIMO. Mark an **X** on each spot that is called to see who will get "SLIMO" first! The winner must get 5 **X**'s across a row.

Mark an **X** on these spaces:

- the **free** spot in the middle of each card
- the product of 7 x 4
- the product of 8 x 7
- the product of 7 x 7
- the product of 8 x 8
- the product of 8 x 9
- the product of 8 x 4
- the product of 5 x 3
- the product of 6 x 7
- the product of 7 x 5
- the product of 9 x 4
- the product of 8 x 1
- the product of 7 x 3

S	L	I	M	O
12	17	31	44	72
4	22	36	56	67
14	19	FREE	47	64
8	28	42	45	75
5	23	34	42	63

Tonight
SLIMO
competition

S	L	I	M	O
7	18	35	48	66
15	21	32	49	72
13	24	FREE	45	70
11	20	33	56	63
6	25	41	60	68

Who won the game? _____

Multiplication

Samantha and Rodney are playing tic-tac-toe. Rodney is **X** and Samantha is **O**. Solve these problems to see who wins! Remember that a **product** is the answer to a multiplication problem.

- Put an **X** on the product of 9 x 2.

- Put an **O** on the product of 9 x 3.

- Put an **X** on the product of 9 x 4.

- Put an **O** on the product of 9 x 5.

- Put an **X** on the product of 9 x 6.

- Put an **O** on the product of 9 x 7.

- Put an **X** on the product of 9 x 8.

- Put an **O** on the product of 9 x 9.

Who won the game? _____

Addition and Subtraction

Mark wants to play tic-tac-toe with you. Write the answers to all the equations. Then, color the three boxes in each game that have the same answers. One math problem has been done for you.

5 − 2 **3**	9 + 11	14 − 4
12 − 5	20 − 17	8 + 4
3 + 12	8 − 4	1 + 2

9 − 4	2 + 6	10 + 5
20 − 6	15 − 9	9 + 8
16 − 4	7 + 5	20 − 8

What is the message on the billboard? Complete the addition and subtraction equations below to find out. Write the letter under each equation on the line (or lines) on the billboard that matches the answer to that math problem.

5 + 2 = _____
S

11 + 9 = _____
A

16 – _____ = 11
H

10 – _____ = 1
T

16 – 2 = _____
E

2 + _____ = 6
Y

11 – 1 = _____
M

7 – _____ = 4
I

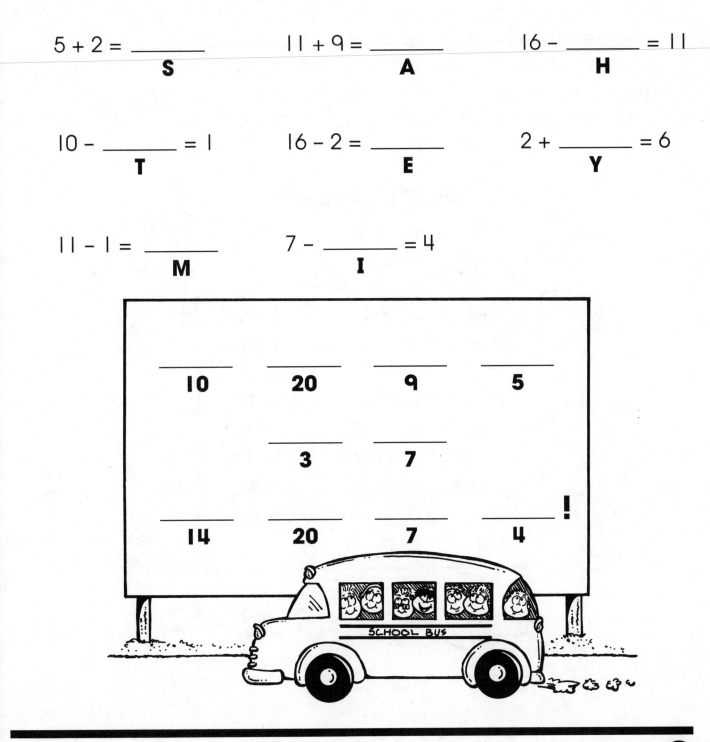

_____   _____   _____   _____
10   20   9   5

_____   _____
3   7

_____   _____   _____   _____ !
14   20   7   4

The monsters love to break secret codes. They also love movies! In fact, they think they know everything about every movie ever made. But they're not as smart as they think!

They have to discover the name of a famous movie song, and you can help them by breaking the secret code below. In the code, every letter stands for a number. Solve the problems on the next page to find out which letter goes in each blank. If all your answers are correct, you'll soon discover the mystery song title!

SECRET CODE KEY

A-5	J-1	S-22
B-8	K-3	T-40
C-2	L-11	U-75
D-0	M-4	V-80
E-6	N-20	W-50
F-10	O-25	X-100
G-12	P-28	Y-90
H-7	Q-30	Z-60
I-9	R-70	

Here are 24 problems. Solve each of them and write down the sums. Then, find the letter in the secret code key that corresponds to each sum. The first one is done for you.

1. $5 + 5 + 5 - 5 =$ ___10___ ___F___

2. $6 + 6 - 4 =$ _____ _____

3. $3 + 2 + 10 - 4 =$ _____ _____

4. $70 - 30 =$ _____ _____

5. $20 + 30 - 41 =$ _____ _____

6. $3 + 2 + 6 =$ _____ _____

7. $3 + 3 + 6 - 1 =$ _____ _____

8. $15 + 15 + 40 =$ _____ _____

9. $10 + 5 + 10 =$ _____ _____

10. $11 - 6 =$ _____ _____

11. $70 - 60 - 4 =$ _____ _____

12. $20 + 4 - 21 =$ _____ _____

13. $20 + 20 + 10 =$ _____ _____

14. $18 - 6 - 6 =$ _____ _____

15. $70 + 30 - 50 =$ _____ _____

16. $10 + 5 + 10 =$ _____ _____

17. $20 + 20 + 30 =$ _____ _____

18. $20 + 10 - 5 =$ _____ _____

19. $18 + 4 - 20 =$ _____ _____

20. $6 + 5 + 10 - 10 =$ _____ _____

21. $12 + 8 - 10 - 3 =$ _____ _____

22. $10 + 10 + 5 =$ _____ _____

23. $40 + 50 =$ _____ _____

24. $16 + 4 + 50 - 70 =$ _____ _____

Write a letter in each blank below. There is one blank for each of the 24 problems. The first one is done for you.

___ ___ ___ ___ ___ ___   ___ ___ ___
 1   16   3   7   18   13   4   21   14

___ ___ ___ ___ ___ ___
23   11   20   6   9   15

___ ___ ___ ___ ___   ___ ___ ___ ___
 2   17   5   19   12   8   22   10   24

Ordinal Numbers

Follow the directions below to discover the mystery word. The puzzle begins on the left with the letter **A**.

- Cross out the ninth letter.
- Cross out the tenth letter.
- Cross out the fifth letter.
- Cross out the second letter.
- Cross out the seventh letter.
- Cross out the sixth letter.

ASHTODYMCR

Write the four letters that are left over:

_____ _____ _____ _____

Unscramble the four letters to spell the mystery word:

_____ _____ _____ _____

Two frogs are racing to the pond. Color one frog green. Color the other frog orange. The race begins behind rock #1. The green frog jumps over 1 rock at a time. The orange frog jumps over 2 rocks at a time. Draw a green **X** on each rock the green frog lands on. Draw an orange **X** on each rock the orange frog lands on.

Which frog reaches the pond first? _____

Even and Odd Numbers

Numbers that are not even are called **odd numbers**. **Odd numbers** cannot be divided into two groups that are exactly the same. Use a blue crayon to color the boxes that contain an **odd number**.

Hint: Use pennies or other small objects to help you count the odd numbers.

12	5	17	11	18
2	4	3	14	20
18	10	19	16	6
8	9	15	1	4

What letter did all the blue boxes form? _____

For an extra challenge, circle all the numbers that are odd.

| 1 | 2 | 3 | 4 | 5 | 6 | 7 | 8 | 9 | 10 |
| 11 | 12 | 13 | 14 | 15 | 16 | 17 | 18 | 19 | 20 |

Rosie is trying to open the safe. But she doesn't know the numbers that will open the lock. You can help her.

Fill in the answers to the mystery math problems. Then, draw an **X** in the **Even** column if the answer is even or in the **Odd** column if it's odd.

Number	Even	Odd
$7 + 3 + 4 =$ _____		
$8 - 5 + 3 =$ _____		
$2 + 2 + 3 =$ _____		
$9 - 3 + 2 =$ _____		
$6 + 2 - 2 =$ _____		

If there are more than 2 odd numbers and fewer than 4 even numbers, then frogs are in the safe.

If there are more than 3 even numbers and fewer than 2 odd numbers, then gold is in the safe.

Circle the treasure Rosie found in the safe.

Addition

Play a game of tic-tac-toe with a friend. You and your friend should each use different-colored crayons. Instead of **X**'s and **O**'s, take turns writing numbers on the squares. The winner is the player who can make three numbers in any row add up to 20. Rows can go down (↓), across (⟶) or diagonally (↗↘). Numbers can be used more than once in a game.

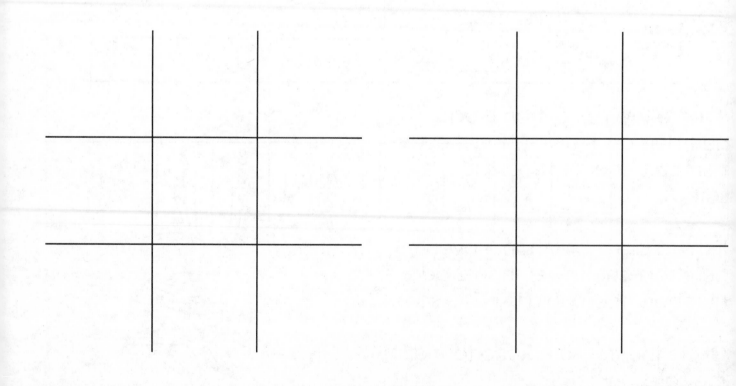

Help the monster complete the problems in the grid below. Color them according to the chart.

If the answer is 3, color the space blue.
If the answer is 4, color the space green.
If the answer is 5, color the space purple.

19 −8 / 4 +9 / 19 −3 / 15 −12	13 −5 / 16 +1 / 5 +2 / 8 −5	4 +4 / 10 +6 / 11 −2 / 16 −3	9 +2 / 10 −10 / 7 +7 / 12 +1	11 −5 / 6 +6 / 12 +2 / 13 −10	9 +1 / 8 +8 / 5 +5 / 11 −8
3 +1	9 −5	12 +9	14 +3	23 −19	20 −16
2 +2	8 −4 / 11 −6 / 13 −9 / 1 +3	16 −12	25 −21	3 +2 / 7 −3 / 12 −8 / 17 −13	15 −11
5 −1	6 −2	19 −15 / 13 −8	16 −11 / 14 −10	18 −14	14 −10

Addition/Subtraction

Begin at the sign that says START. Move from a number to a plus or minus sign, then to another number as shown. You can only move to a square that touches the square you are in. Find a path that leads to the answer, which is marked EXIT.

One Monster Maze has been done for you. Help the monsters solve the other one!

START

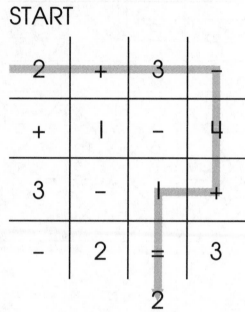

2	+	3	–
+	l	–	4
3	–	l	+
–	2	=	3

2

EXIT

START

4	–	2	+
–	l	+	3
4	+	2	–
3	–	=	l

4

EXIT

Begin at the sign that says START. Find a path that leads to the answer.

START

6	+	6	–
+	1	–	3
2	–	4	+
–	5	=	1

5
EXIT

START

8	–	4	+
–	3	+	2
5	+	1	–
–	7	=	4

6
EXIT

Addition/Subtraction

Vinnie and Vivian lost their house keys. They know they left the keys at a place they visited today. They've been to the Monster Cafe, the Witch's House, the Elf Cave and the Troll Tree House. Use the clues in the box below and the map on the next page to help them get to the place where they left their keys.

1. Go to the number that is less than 20 and made with two 1's.

2. Then, subtract 4 from that number, and add 7.

3. Next, add 2 six times to that number.

4. Then, go to the number that is a reversal of the number you are on.

5. Now, subtract 10 six times from that number.

6. Next, add 7 to that number, and subtract 8.

7. After that, add 20 to that number.

8. Then, subtract 6 three times from that number.

9. Finally, add 7 to that number, then add a 0 to the end.

Put a marker in the START square. Solve each problem in the clue box, and move your marker to the number box that matches each answer. You may go in any direction.

If you answer all the clues correctly, you will land on the place where Vinnie and Vivian left their keys.

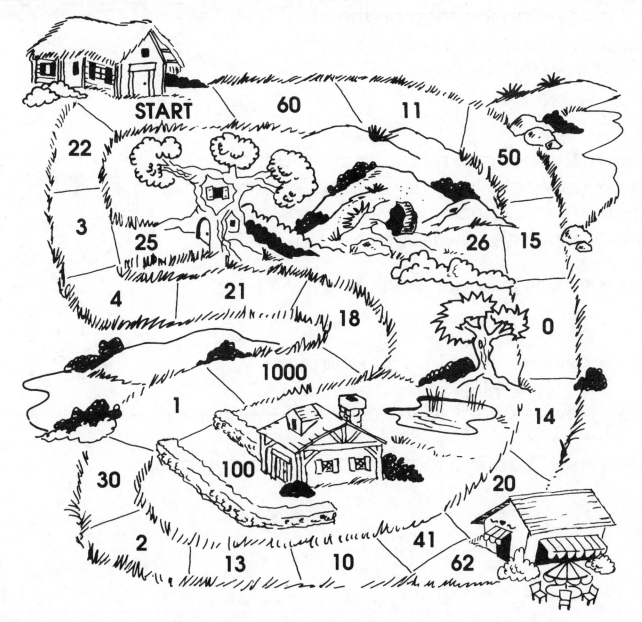

Where did the monsters leave their keys? _____

Look at the two trains below. They are named Casey and Clank.

CLANK   CASEY

Which train is shorter? _____

Which train is longer? _____

Cory the conductor needs to construct a
brand-new train. He is going to name this train
Chuck. Help Cory by following the clues below
and drawing his new train in the box.

- Chuck is longer than Casey.

- Chuck is shorter than Clank.

- Chuck has an engine pulling an
  even number of rail cars.

When you compare the **height** of objects, you tell how **tall** or how **short** they are. Look at Timmy's action figures. Then, circle the answers to the questions.

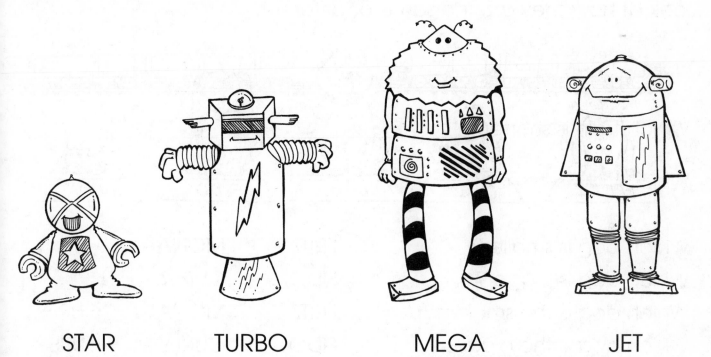

STAR   TURBO   MEGA   JET

Which toy is shorter?   STAR   MEGA

Which toy is taller?   TURBO   JET

Which action figure is Timmy's newest one? Use these clues to find out.

- It is not the tallest or the shortest action figure.

- It is the action figure that is the taller of the remaining two toys.

Write its name: _____

Size/Logic

Look at all the dogs who entered the dog show. Some dogs are big. Some dogs are small. Compare the sizes of the dogs. Then, circle the correct answers below. When you **compare** things, you look at how they are the same or different.

Which dog is smaller?	FRITZ	MONA	
Which dog is bigger?	FIDO	CURLY	
Which dog is the smallest?	FRITZ	MONA	CURLY
Which dog is the biggest?	FIDO	CURLY	DUKE
Which dogs are the same size?	DUKE	FRITZ	FIDO

Now, use these clues to find out which dog won first prize in the dog show.

Hint: Put an **X** on each dog that did not win.

- The winner is not the biggest dog.

- Neither of the two dogs that are the same size is the winner.

- The winner is not the smallest dog.

The first prizewinner is: _____

Karen lives in an apartment building that has 10 floors. Find out which floor Karen lives on by following the clues below.

Hint: Put an **X** on each floor that she does not live on.

- Karen does not live on the bottom floor.

- She does not live on the top floor.

- She lives somewhere between the 2nd floor and the 8th floor.

- She does not live on the 4th floor.

- She does not live on the floor above the 4th floor.

- She does not live on the 7th floor.

- There are two floors left. Karen lives on the floor with the higher number.

Karen lives on the _____ floor.
(Write the ordinal number as a numeral.)